MY ENCOUNTER with **MINI INDIA** in MUMBAI CUSTOMS

- A MEMOIR -

BY

HEMESH CHHABRA

First Published in April 2023

ISBN: 978-93-5741-122-6

BLUEROSE PUBLISHERS
www.BlueRoseONE.com
info@bluerosepublishers.com
+91 8882 898 898

Cover Design:
Bhushan Chhabra

Typographic Design:
Namrata Saini

Distributed by: BlueRose, Amazon, Flipkart

About Author

Hemesh Chhabra born in 1962 in a Digambar Jain Family, in Jaipur, Rajasthan. He did his schooling in the famous Mahavir School of Jaipur and graduation from Commerce college, Rajasthan University, where he also attended classes on Journalism and Law. After doing few short span services in 5 different Banks and Financial Institutions, ultimately, he joined Mumbai Customs as Preventive Officer in 1986. Perfection, Self-improvement and to acquire knowledge of any subject has always been his **IKIGAI**. During his service in Mumbai Customs, he did short courses in Film Script writing and Film Direction. He also did his "post graduate diploma in Human Rights" for which he wrote "Jainism and Human Rights" as Master Thesis, duly accepted by Indian Institute of Human Rights. He is a strong proponent of Human Rights which was quite noticeable during his entire service career in the Customs and Indirect Taxes. He penned this memoir about his insight of experiencing a paradigm shift of Mumbai customs into its mini- India characteristic. He retired from the central Government service in 2022 as Assistant Commissioner and now lives in Mumbai.

Acknowledgement

Writing a book about the experiences of 28 years Long service career is a surreal process. Although this period of my life was filled with many ups and downs, my time in Mumbai Customs was worth it. I'm forever indebted to my Batchmates, my colleagues in Mumbai Customs, my friends and my Family for their support and encouragement in my long service career. My time in Mumbai Customs wouldn't have been made possible without their wholehearted support and then this book would not have been in your hand. Thanks a lot, my dear **Confreres.........**

Writing a book is harder than I thought and more rewarding than I could have ever imagined. None of this would have been possible without my wife Sangeeta. She was the first person who encouraged me to write a book on my service experiences after my Retirement. She stood by me during every struggle, service matters and rendered her full support to enable me, to perform my official duties efficiently and punctually and conceiving this book. Thanks a lot, my dear **Sangu.........**

Writing a good book, completing it and getting it published is not possible without the continuous and wholehearted support of near and dear ones. I am especially thankful to my awesome Son **Bhushan** who was always available there for me to assist, to recall the experiences, to edit with keen insight, in bringing my service experiences to life. He was as important to this book getting done as I was. Thank you so much, dear **Bhushan**..........

Contents

Prologue

किताब -ए-जिंदगी के वरक पलटे ऐसे,
जैसे पलकें मेरी, बेसाख्ता आमादगी से झपके....

बे-बहा मुम्बई कस्टम्स की मुलाजमत जैसे,
मुक्कमल की मैंने, नुमाइंदा भारत से रुबरु होके...

I retired on Superannuation on 31-08-2022 after completing more than 36 years of my service in Central Government, with Customs and Central Excise (Indirect Taxes). Now after retirement since I have leisure time, I often reminisce important events of my peregrination in the Department as if a pelicula continuously moving in my memory like running a movie in a kaleidoscope.

Out of 36 years I spent 28 years with Mumbai Customs. In fact, it is "Indian Customs, Mumbai". At the time of my joining, it was referred as Bombay Customs, but after the change of the name from Bombay to Mumbai, it is now referred as Mumbai Customs. Therefore, I have used the term "Mumbai Customs" throughout in this book. Merely a reference of Mumbai Customs, flashes me back to those 28 years when I was working for Mumbai Customs. It makes me nostalgic.

Now today when I look behind, working with Mumbai Customs, it seems as if most of the time, one area of my life was in a good place and rarely another one went disarray. I feel now I have better understanding of my duties which I performed while working with Mumbai Customs. Continuation of a plethora of scenes flashing into my mind is forcing me to convert these scenes into words. My fascination to share my service experiences of finding 'Mini -India within the fence of Mumbai Customs' too has been the driving force, which culminated in the publication of this book.

This book may provide an account and nature of preventive service in Mumbai Customs of the period of 1986 to 2014 for those who are interested in it.

I am sure that this book would stir the service-memories of my colleagues, of my batchmates, of my seniors and of all other confederates of Mumbai Customs, who go through this book.

I hope my endeavour shall not be considered narcissistic, rather it would be taken as a shared experience for eudemonistic happiness. I am pouring my spirit of those 28 years in this book and hope God lead the way.

HEMESH CHHABRA

My Entry Into Mumbai Customs

Almost 37 years back, in march 1986, I, then a young lad of 24 yrs., alighted at Bombay Central station with a dilemma in my mind to Join Mumbai Customs as preventive officer or not. I belonged to Jaipur and was working with Indian Overseas Bank in Jaipur. Though I was quite satisfied with the 10 to 5 office life and happily growing tummy, yet sometimes I got bored with monotonous life. Therefore, I had applied for the combined examination which was to be conducted by Staff Selection Commissions (Previously known as Subordinate Services Commission) for the post of Income Tax Inspector, / Central Excise Inspector/ Preventive Officer (PO) of Customs and Examiner in 1984. Fortunately, I was selected for the post of Preventive Officer. I received appointment letter from the office of Bombay Customs in January' 1986. And thus, had come to Bombay (Now Mumbai). I had been called to New Customs House, Ballard Estate, Bombay for the purpose of Joining Customs.

Before coming to Bombay, I had taken first hand details of nature of duty from some of the officers working in Central excise in Jaipur and from the people who had some knowledge of the customs.

Then I came to the given address and saw the magnificent three storied, "New Custom House", Bombay. I was very much thrilled with the thought that this building could be my work place and headquarter. In New Custom House at the ground Floor Control Room and then in the corridor at the second Floor opposite Establishment Section, I met some of my batchmates, who were directly recruited pan India as preventive officers by SSC. However, I was astounded when informed by some of them that though, few of our batchmates had joined Customs three-four months back but afterwards Customs had stopped our remaining batch officers to join in customs and that if wished we could join in Central Excise. All of us were not only nervous but very furious also since we all had come to join only in customs as Preventive Officers and were not ready to join as Inspector of Central Excise. It also transpired that under the circumstances, few days back some of our batchmates had already joined in Central Excise office at Churchgate Office. But one thing was clear that all of us were insisting to join only in Bombay Customs as we were given appointment letter by the Customs. Majority of us were inexperienced and new in Mumbai. We all had come from different parts of India, selected by SSC, under whose recommendation we were given appointment letters by the appointing authority of customs. How the Customs could denounce its own official letter...? The establishment Section's dealing ministerial staff, Mr. Desai was not of any help as he had been ordered not to allow us to give our papers and join. What was the way......!!

One of my batchmates was local Mumbaikar, he knew about the regional office of the SSC in Bombay. He suggested that we should go to the SSC Office. We all immediately agreed and in a distraught group reached to Army Navy Building, in which the regional office of SSC was situated. We found that the Regional Director was a lady (I cannot remember her name). We met her in her chamber. She was a very kind and considerate person, listened to us calmly and assured us that she would definitely do something and asked us to meet her later and busied herself doing phone calls to Delhi SSC Office. Next day, when we met her, she stated that there had been some confusion with regard to our joining in customs and simultaneously gave us good news that we could join in customs and that necessary orders have been sent to appointing authority in New custom House. So, we came back to New Custom House, where we contacted the establishment section. They had the modified orders and were ready to allow all of us to join, along with the officers who had earlier joined in

Central Excise. But before joining we were to pass the physical fitness test, like fulfilment of minimum height criteria (For PO it was minimum 153 CMs), weight, chest expansion, and that not having any Achromatopsia (Colour blindness) etc. Few of my batchmates could not pass the tests (other than Height) in first attempt but later they could succeed. Cycling skill was also a necessity for a PO during those days. So, we had to pass the cycling test, which was conducted at Five Gardens, Matunga/Wadala. The Customs colony at Five Gardens, which I noticed while giving cycling test, fascinated me a lot and that time I thought that it was a colony worth living in. I passed both tests, i.e., physical fitness and cycling, very easily. I must confess that though I had appeared in both the tests still I had not made up my mind with regard to joining Bombay Customs due to the uncertainties at the initial stage and I had begun to think dropping the Idea of joining Customs. That was my first- stage encounter with the Mini India Nature of Mumbai Customs.

My batchmates were consisting a major chunk from Orissa and others from different states of India. I also met many other officers who were locally promoted from the cadre of ministerial staff and were mainly Mumbaikars, in true sense. Then I had the opportunity to meet my senior officers, beautifully clad in the pristine white uniform, giving "कड़क salute" to their seniors. ("Kadak salutation" I learnt during my training). Some of my batchmates who had earlier joined the 'customs' had got their uniforms sewn and were wearing the same and getting the kadak salute from khaki dressed Havildars & Sepoys. They had also got their gate fold I-Card and were showing proudly to each other like a police officer showed his I-card to an evildoer in olden Hindi movies.

There was moment to moment changes in my thoughts inside the humongous structure of New Customs House and it was clear enough to push me into thinking weather the jump in my career was duly required. While contemplating my thoughts I also saw a work environment never seen before. Khaki Uniform clad Havaldars/Sepoys, saluting White Uniform Clad officers. Officers Saluting their Seniors, which then I had no idea on how to differentiate. After a keen observation and remembering the details given to me by the Central Excise Officers at Jaipur, while collecting the information about the duties of a customs Officer. I figured out that the epaulettes on the shoulders of their uniform showed the hierarchy, position of the officer. Long queues of well-dressed people waiting in line outside specific Cabins, Havaldars on their toes, Sepoys running around and fetching files, papers, tea, snacks and other items for officers sitting in their cabins. These were the first few glimpses of my entry into this whole new world of

Customs Department. These all things put a great impact on me and were gradually making up in my subconscious mind to join Bombay Customs. Eventually, while peeing in the third-floor toilet opposite floating room, where we were directed to sit, looking through the oculus-window, I saw the vastness of the Arabian sea, its greyish blue water in which many naval ships were anchored, a partly cloudy sky, and a fresh breeze flowing, it all fascinated me a lot since I had come from a dry state Rajasthan which doesn't have a sea coast. That point of time was my Eureka moment. It was this moment which now defines my whole life, personal and professional, and it was at this very moment, while taking a leak in that 3rd floor Gents Toilet that I took final decision to join Bombay Customs. And thus, getting rid of my initial dilemma of joining customs or not. It has been almost 37yrs now and I still cannot forget the instance when I had the alacrity and had made up my mind to join Mumbai customs as Preventive officer. The sea still symbolizes my life and my service career which I had passed during the 28 years of my service with the Mumbai Customs.

I joined, Bombay customs on 11-03-1986 as preventive officer (PO). And on the same day at 12:30 pm I took the oath of allegiance to the Constitution of India, before the then Assistant Collector of Customs, in his Cabin situated at the third

Floor of New Custom House. During the oath and just after taking the oath, I found a change in me. I realised that I had become the part of the Government and as a responsible Government Servant I would be required to perform my official duties loyally and sincerely.

After that, I, along with some of my batchmates went to the Abu Moosa Tailor Shop, situated opposite Red Gate Indira Dock, on Walchand Hirachand Marg and ordered for urgent two white Uniforms of PO, two pairs of Sea- Customs epaulettes and other accoutrements.

After joining, I along with my batchmates had to struggle for getting the accommodation. There were no departmental quarters available for junior officers like us. Almost all of us, my Batchmates, were new in Bombay and mostly no one had any acquaintances close enough to provide shelter. So far, many of us had been living in some medium category low-cost Hotels or Guest Houses, but it was not going to be the lasting solution, after our joining in Mumbai Customs. We had to run pillar to post to get the place where we could sleep and do our morning routines. So, many of us arranged a small flat on sharing basis at "ANTOP HILL". I shared a flat with three of my batchmates at Kane Nagar, Antop Hill. Antop Hill was mainly a Government Housing Complex, divided in seven Sectors and maintained by CPWD. In Antop Hill people belonging from all over India were staying and I befriended with many of them. Later I shared five Garden Quarter with one of my Maharashtrian Colleagues Mr. A. M. Panchami, till I was allotted a quarter in my own name in the Customs Colony at Five Gardens.

Training

A training schedule was fixed, In the month of April 1986, and I, along with a part of my batchmates, was nominated for orientation/Induction training course, at Mole Station, Ballard Pier, Indira Dock, Green Gate, near New Customs House. Our training instructors were Mr. Q.S. Kazi (then a very senior superintendent) and Mr. A.U. Kohok (Senior P.O)

Mr Kohok had a very loud and coercive voice. All the time he beat his brains out to make the novice officers physically strong and fit for doing the hard duties which as a PO we were to perform in the Department in the forthcoming time. And of course, he was right as we were going to do really hard duties including 12 hours night duty at various gates and later on at Airport and in R &. I. I must say that he was successful in growing us as hard-working POs. Mr. kohok gave us the training of Parade/March Past. He insisted that we must carry a straight posture all the time. I did not have much difficulty in this training as I had participated in March Past during my school days. However, some of my other batchmates were finding it difficult to keep up paces and hand positions synchronized with other paraders. After fifteen days training, there was desired improvement in all the trainees. Mr. Kohok, also taught us how to salute seniors in customs and that customs way of saluting resembled with Navy Salutation, in which the palm of right hand is brought to the forehead almost touching the brim of the peak cap or eyebrow, keeping the palm facing downward at almost 90-degree angle to the forehead with synchronizing the crisp and quick movement of right foot, lifting it 9" - 12" and then slamming it on the ground, juxtaposing the other foot and making a sharp thud sound. He said "ये होता है कड़क सैल्यूट" while demonstrating the same. Later I hand saluted in this way to my seniors throughout my service in Mumbai customs and even afterwards also in Central Excise/GSt also, though the action of salutation was different in Cen Ex/GST. **Old habits die hard.**

Our senior training Instructor Supdt. Qamar S. Kazi was a kind, low voiced, sympathetic but stubborn, a very seasoned and respect- commanding officer. Most of us, being trainees, in a whole new environment, were very much impressed by him. He explained us the duties and working of POs, its importance, and how to use and implement the laws while doing the duties. He taught us to accept the differentiation of ethnicity, of caste, creed, color, race, while working as PO. He taught us how to respect seniors and how to earn respect from Juniors.

He gave us lectures on how to write a Pachanama, what are precautions to be taken before, during and at the end of drawing Panchanama. He elaborated that we, the customs preventive officers were the first and the last government officers to deal with international passengers & tourist, and thus had great responsibility to represent India in a graceful manner and at the same time implementing the requisite laws and rules. I was most enthralled by his pedagogy, especially the way he ingrained a sense of belonging to the department, in the minds of all the trainees, which always remained in our subconscious mind throughout our career. Because of that we referred Bombay customs as "our Bombay Customs" (Later Mumbai Customs). I feel it is an honour to me when Mr. Kazi, now octogenarian, happened to see me, after 35yrs of the training, in the marriage function of one of my batchmate's son and immediately remembered me and called me "अये लम्बे बाल वाला" as he fondly called me during the induction training.

During the Training it became clear to me that there were two wings of customs' administration. One was Appraising wing and the other was preventive wing. The Appraising wing of Customs dealt with the examination of Import/export cargo and ancillary work thereof adhering to Customs Act, & Rules, implementing and charging customs Duty as per the Customs Tarif Act and that they were not assigned any particular uniform. The officers appointed through SSC for the appraising wing were called Examiners.

Whereas preventive branch, as the name suggested, worked for the prevention of duty evasion and smuggling of prohibited & restricted goods. As such, it was assigned the prophylactic duty at various entry & Exit Points (Gates of Customs controlled and notified Areas) to thwart any attempt of duty evasion and smuggling. It also supplemented the activities of other departments in enforcing the Customs Act and other allied acts, work related to arrival and departure of vessels and air crafts, discharge landing, and clearance of imported and warehoused goods, shipment and transshipment of the goods at docks, airports and other Land stations. Even in the case of regular import and export of goods through the normal channel, though the procedure connected therewith were attended by appraising Wing, it was the preventive wing which ensured the total observance of law by the trade and public by effecting proper checks at the point of entry /exit. In short there was no aspect of customs functioning with which the preventive service was not directly or indirectly associated.

Since the passenger traffic at Airport and sea Port could be a channel for duty evasion and smuggling activities, the white Uniformed Preventive officers were posted at the Ports to deter the delinquents. In furtherance of the same, the examination of Passengers Baggage was assigned to Preventive Branch and therefore Officers of Preventive wing were eligible for posting at Airport as ACO (Air Customs Officers) and ACS (Air Customs Superintendent) and were required to wear pristine white Uniform, while performing their normal official duties. The preventive officer of customs was the first person to greet any visitor and the last to see him off. In the process he had to shoulder dual responsibility. On the one hand he had to conduct himself as an ambassador of India and on the other hand he had to ensure the proper observance of the law of the land.

To cultivate and gather Intelligence on duty evasion and smuggling activities, investigation thereof and carry out the prosecution proceedings were also important tasks given to the preventive wing. Preventive officers were not required to wear White Uniform while working as Intelligence Officers, obviously to obtain fruitful results.

The officers appointed through SSC for preventive wing were called Preventive Officers.

During my training I also came to know that promotion prospects of preventive wing in Mumbai Customs were very dim and that the POs were lesser fortunate than Examiners, as far as promotions were concerned and that it could take a Preventive Officer even 20 years to be promoted as Superintendent of Customs (Preventive), whereas an examiner could be promoted as Appraiser within 8-9 years.

Both the Customs wings functioned separately and there was least interaction between the two, while doing the customs work. However, there was an option... POs could opt for promotion as Appraiser as per the seniority, which was also more than 18 years of service, required that time. Later the period for promotion was reduced and I got my promotion as Superintendent of Customs (Preventive) (Supdt. P) after 16 years of service in the year 2002, whereas the Examiners who also joined Mumbai Customs along with me had got their promotion in the year 1993. No special training was imparted to us after promotion to Supdt., though various trainings were given later on different subjects/ themes, mostly at NACEN (National Academy of Customs, Excise and Narcotics) (Now NACIN: National Academy of Customs, Indirect Taxes and Narcotics), Regional Training Institute, Bhandup. However, our field experience was the father of all the Trainings.

During the course of my Induction Training, I also realized, that even though all of us trainees were bound by one confinement to work for Customs Department but in reality, we all were very different people from very different regions of India. All of our likes and dislikes were different. Our Deities were different, our day-to-day routine was different, or culture was different, our eating habits were different. Communication skills were different, Festivals were different and a whole lot more. This is where I learned, that although we were of about same age with the same goal in mind but we all were very different people and I had suddenly found myself coming in contact with not only just Rajasthani - Marwaris but with the whole lot of Indians and this exposure was very enthralling and making my mental aptitude widened.

Postings

There were various and different types of postings for POs in Bombay Customs. A posting order, called "General Shift", was issued biannually by Assistant Collector, PG (Preventive General) (Now Assistant Commissioner/ ACPG) PSO (Posting Section Office). As per the norms, the "Shift" was supposed to be issued every six months but it was never brought out on time. One of the main reasons for "Shift" not coming out on time was the pressure on ACPG/ PSO for good postings by the resourceful officers, who were usually referred as stalwarts or officers having **"VASILA"** (वसीला). **"Vasila"** could be anyone, senior bosses, Bosses in Delhi, political bigwigs or any other VIPs, who could effectively put pressure on the higher authorities empowered to influence the Posting Order and to post some particular officer at some particular place of Posting. For one particular posting there could be many aspirants, resulting in delay of the "Shift". The Hindi proverb एक अनार सौ बिमार was befitting to explain the circumstance. "Postings" like Airport, R & I were given for two years, in more or less time bound manner, to those who fulfilled the conditions of minimum service and cooling- off period. There were some postings for one year period like ACC, Air Line Bonds, Disposal & Bond Posting. (ACC posting was made for two years later) There were some deputation postings like SEEPZ (Santacruz Electronics Export Processing Zone) posting and many other cost Recovery postings (where the entities, getting full time services of PO(s), were to reimburse the amount to Govt. towards the salary and perks of the PO(s). The rest of the postings were given for a period of six months. For non-resourceful officers, in most of the cases, place of posting was given at random and at the wish and whims of PSO. Out of the available postings, some postings were highly demanded like A Division posting, which included Boarding Office, and UB (Unaccompanied Baggage) Centre. Other demand postings were division Posting, (Division B to F Division), CFSs (Container freight Stations) like MOD, STP, and Wharf gate postings like Ferry Wharf, and postings in Disposal, Bond, Air Lines Bonds etc. and common officers like me hardly got these postings. Then there were many normal postings like Frere Basin, Hay Bunder, Haji Bunder, Sasoon Docks etc. which were neither demanded nor dejected. Then there were postings where no officers wanted to work like Control Room Posting, Lakri (लकड़ी) Bunder Posting, Apollo Bunder, Wadi Bunder Postings etc.

As far as Airport, ACC and R & I postings were concerned, the job of the PSO was only to depute the required number of Officers to these places in a fairly time bound manner. The local postings at Airport, ACC and R & I were not in the hands of PSO, and were made by the concerned Admin Section.

Soon after the training, we trainee officers, all slowly and steadily drifted apart into our postings, some were favored into certain postings and some got which no one wanted. We all had entered a world full of opportunities and the vastness of Arabian sea started to feel small.

ACC: I was posted at Sahar Air Caro Complex (ACC). For me who had earlier worked at a Bank Branch, having limited space. ACC was huge Shed on the tarmac and, joining the Runway of the Sahar Airport (As Mumbai International Airport was called that time) for a workplace and my experiences in New customs House felt smaller as far as Area was concerned. At Air Cargo Complex I saw the huge consignments of Import Export General Cargo, Import export of Perishable cargo. I learnt to examine the same from my seniors. As I was the most Junior officer, I was not given the Examination of the Unaccompanied Baggage/ Personal Effects, which were imported by the passengers coming on TR (Transfer of Residence).On TR there was concessional Rate of leviable Customs Duty, on fulfillment of certain conditions. In one of the cases where the unaccompanied Baggage was being examined by a senior PO, more than 1400 video Cassettes were found in the personal effects of the transferee. Since I was Junior, I was assigned to watch the contents of the Video Cassettes. To ensure that it did not have any objectionable contents, like blue film or anything concerning threat to safety and economy of India. So, a VCP (Video Cassette Player) was arranged in the MMTC Strong Room, where a 21" inches Color TV was available and where POs were deputed to keep an account of precious and semi-precious cargos' import export. For four days I just enjoyed those Video cassettes containing many south Indian Regional Films, religious discourses, health tips etc. and nothing objectional was noticed by me. As an ex-Bank employee, it was really enjoyable for me, since in Bank all the time I had dealt only with the figures while writing the Day Book. As a junior PO It was a joy to watch the films as doing official duty.

After some time, in Cargo I was posted in "Batch". There were three batches consisting of 12 POs & Supdts. in each Batch. The duties in Batch were of two shifts of 12 hours each i.e. 8 am to 8 pm and 8 pm to 8 am on Day-Night-Off pattern. In the Batch, my duty was to sign the green colored triplicate copy of the Shipping Bills giving "shipment allowed" endorsement as per one of the mandatory requirements under CA-62 (Customs Act-62), after verification with cargo EGM (Export General

Manifest), to load the examined and customs cleared cargo on the cargo aircrafts called Freighters. That time all the Shipping Bills were manually prepared by the Exporters or their CHAs, and submitted to Customs. Since, by then ICES i.e., Indian Customs EDI (Electronic Data Interchange) System had not been introduced. My other important duty was to escort precious and semi-precious sealed Cargo from MMTC Strong Room, situated in the export Shed next to our Cabin, to the Flights and occasionally examination of perishable cargo in the big Shed called "APEDA" (for Agricultural and Processed Food Products Export Development Authority). The APEDA Shed was a hugely crowded place and all the times, apart from Customs Officers of middle ranks, the Importers, Exporters, their hundreds of CHAs (Customs House Agents), employees of other Agencies, like Airport Authorities, Air Lines, quarantine staff, transporters, loaders, Hand-Cart walls, Janitorial work force were found running here and there. It took me some time to adjust with the crowd and work efficiently at ACC.

I am hemmed and hawed to say that I was not getting cordial welcome from some of my senior colleagues who always reminded me that our batch was encroacher in Bombay Customs. Apart from this, by then I had become home sick, since it was the first time for me to live away from my mother, other relatives and friends. So, I wanted to go to my native place, Jaipur, on leave. I wrote an EL Application and approached to my admin Supdt., gave him a Kadak Salute and explained my purpose of coming to him. Without seeing the application, he just threw it and said It could not be sanctioned. I was shocked and bewildered, as I was mentally tired. I immediately went to AC (Assistant Collector) Admin Mr. Sachdev. AC Sachdev was a recently recruited direct AC and just three to four years older to me. He listened to me calmly and sanctioned my EL then and there. I brought the same and gave it to the Admin Supdt. After seeing the Leave sanctioned by the AC Admin, the Admin Supdt., (who was a Sardarji, clearly on the wrong side of Fifties), got furious and shouted at me that how dared I went to AC directly, when he had rejected the leave. I again explained him my situation very politely. He was not convinced, yet, he could not do anything as Leave had already been sanctioned by AC. But he developed an animosity against me and not only he created many hurdles for me but also vilified against me to other senior officers, during my later working in ACC. Yet, there were many good senior officers also, especially Mohammedan Officers, who supported me morally. Then there, was another Sardarji, a very cool & Calm senior officer, an Indian Hockey Olympian, Mr. Iqbal Jit Singh Grewal, who was very helpful to me. He even used to give me lift on his Bajaj Scooter for return journey from Cargo to

Antop Hill (14 Kms). He drove the scooter very fast and I used to be very fearful but the same time appreciated his control over the fast driven scooter, like he controlled Hockey Ball while playing Hockey for India.

An Elevated Transport Vehicle(ETV), an automatic Exim cargo packages movement system, was recently installed in ACC for faster loading and unloading of Exim Cargo. In one of the night, Collector Airport, who was also the jurisdictional head of Air Cargo, came to inspect the ETV, and was taking opinion of customs officers posted there with regard to the functioning of the ETV and how it was helping in faster loading- unloading of EXIM Cargo packages. I don't remember the context but during the conversation he commented, 'I wish I would have been a PO" It was a big encouragement for me as a junior PO.

I also remember one incidence which I would like to share that during my ACC Tenure A giant Recording System was imported by the evergreen "Dev Anand". His son Suneil Anand, whose Film "Anand Aur Anand" had just been released, had come to get the customs clearance. For it was my first encounter of any film personality after joining Mumbai Customs, I felt elated.

During my Air Cargo Posting I came across new things almost every day and night duty. While examining the Perishable cargo and watching the general Exim cargo kept in the Shed and which were to be examined by the Appraisers/Examiners of the Customs Appraising wing. I was also amazed, some days before the EID, seeing the consignments of tens of thousands of He-Goats (बकरे), which were to be exported to Gulf Countries, specially to Saudi Arabia. Those बकरे were wadded in the specially hired Freighters. Those were jaw-dropping scenes for me, being a Jain.

Needless to say, that the EXIM Cargo Consignments belonged to PAN India Exporters and importers and then their CHAs, (Customs House Agents) Airlines Staff, my seniors, my colleagues, with all of whom I had been interacting regularly, belonged to almost every part of India, and who were indirectly communicating their culture to me. Eventually, I completed my tenure of one year (As it was that time, Now the tenure is two years) at ACC with a lot of experience and having a glimpse of mini-India.

Mazgaon Dock MFG. Bond: After Air Cargo Posting, I was posted in Mazagaon Dock & Alcock Yard for six months, for a preventive vigil and accounting of Bonded imported goods. Mazagaon Ship Building Yard was the India's biggest manufacturer of ships, frigates and submarines. As far as my memory goes,

I remember that one submarine INS "Shalki" (शल्की) and one frigate INS "Kuthar" (कुठार) along with other ships were under construction and the movements of many import, re-export consignments of their parts and accessories were frequently taking place. I used to take rounds in the construction area and wondered in my mind the vastness and technicalities being used to construct a frigate and ship.

My Superintendents were Mr. R. C. Kingsford and B.A. D'Mellow. Mr. Kingsford was very considerate and understanding gentleman. He was very fond of solving Crossword Puzzles, published in the "Times of India" Mid-Day and "The Afternoon" and whenever we had free time, all the officers engaged ourselves in solving the crossword in his cabin, and almost daily we could solve it completely. He taught me many new words.

During my stint at Mazagaon Dock, I got married.

Floating: After Mazagaon Docks I was posted in "Floating". Floating POs were mainly given the Gate Postings. In those days there were 09 gates in the three docks, viz. Indira Dock (IDK), Victoria Dock (VDK) and. Princess Dock (PDK). These gates were manned round the clock 24 X 7 X 365. In floating, around 54-55 POs were posted to man these gates and for other occasional work like escorting of non-customs cleared goods to and from various Bonded

Warehouses. Floating POs were also posted as temporary substitutes of the officers, (who went on long leave), posted at other postings including Division Postings, It is pertinent to mention here that there were Six Division Offices viz. A Division, B Div. C Div. D Div. E div. and F Division. These Divisions had their earmarked jurisdictions in the Docks area. In the day time Division Supdts. were the supervising In-Charge of the Gate POs, posted on the gates which were coming under their respective jurisdictions. Though the Floating POs were under the direct administrative control of the PSO. The POs were posted at Docks Gates mainly in two shifts duties: 9am to 6 pm and 6pm to 9 am, to keep a watch on the movement of Import export cargo and to ensure that all the customs formalities were complied with properly before crossing the gate. To relieve the outgoing Gate PO and to be relieved by the incoming Gate PO on time inculcated a sense of strict punctuality in all of the POs and later it became the norm. Floating POs' posting order was issued on daily basis at 6 pm by the PSO. All the floating POs were required to check up their next day's posting at 6 pm. One -one copy of the Daily posting order was made available at Control Room, at B division Office, at White Gate VDK and at main Gate PDK. There was a functional telephone land line at White gate VDK and most of the officers posted at other gates and on Off-Duty used to enquire their next day's posting either from the white Gate PO or the control room officer or from B division. Around 8-10 Supdts. were also kept in Floating as supervisory and controlling authority of Floating POs in the night time. During Night Duties, anyone of the floating superintendents was posted to make surprise visits at any time, mostly odd hours, to check whether the Gate POs, at the Docks Gates and at various bunders like Apollo Bunder, Brick Bunder, Lakri Bunder Hay Bunder, Haji Bunder, Wadi Bunder, and at wharfs like Sassoon Dock. Ferry Wharf, as well as at CFSs' (Container Freight Stations, which were extended arms of the Bombay Docks) Gates (like MOD, STP, Frere Basin and up to Wadala Incinerator Plot.) were alert on duty or not. The night visiting floating Supdt. sat in B Division office and in the morning, he used to prepare a report of incidences occurred in the night and timing of his visits to various gates during the night duty. The report was required to be submitted to AC(PG) on the next day. Gate PO maintained a Station Diary in which he had to make the details of the time of attending and leaving the Duty, the important items received from the relieved PO and any important event happened during his duty time. Gate PO was supposed to make an entry in the station Diary even for leaving for the toilet, lest in his absence from the Chowki, visiting Supdt. might come for the visit. One of the Night visiting floating Supdt. was a fearsome Supdt. Shri Mehta. He was very strict and he did not like any PO sitting in the cabin/Chowki. He wanted that all the time POs must stand outside the Chowki to keep a preventive watch on every movement. We used to be scared, whenever knew that Mehta Sahab was for the Visit. Gate officers always enquired from the Control Room Officer and other Gate POs about the movement of Visiting Supdt., especially when Mehta Saab was posted for night visit. In one sad incidence one of our batchmate Mukesh Kumar was treaded over by a moving crane, when he was cycling back in hurry from a nearby gate at MOD, in a rainy night, to come back to his Chowki, as Mehta Sahab was about to visit his chowki.

There was Green Gate IDK at the southernmost end of the Mumbai Docks. It was specifically meant for the passing of the Crew Members of the Ships and for the passengers whenever any Luxury Liner passenger ship arrived at Ballard Pier Indira Dock. In my time one of the biggest Luxury Liners "Golden Odyssey" came to Bombay Port and I had the opportunity to see the wealthy international passengers coming to Bombay as tourists, and envied their sumptuous excursion.

A little further towards north, there was Grey Gate IDK, specifically allotted for the movement of Unaccompanied Baggage cleared from UB Centre.

A little further, there was Red Gate Indira Dock, near B Division Office through which almost all the

Customs Senior Officers and other Customs House Staff passed through on their vehicles, and the officer posted there was supposed to salute them, so he had to be open-eyed all the time. There had been many instances when Officer posted at Red Gate was given warning for not saluting a passing by senior Officer, and who was stopped for "Pass" check by the police sepoy posted at the gate.

Further there was Blue Gate IDK, for the passing out of Customs Cleared Imported goods arrived on the vessels anchored in IDK. There was Chakri near the vehicular Gate. All the Docks-workers used this Chakri to go to the VT Station (Now CSMT), which was very nearby to it.

Then there was Victoria Dock and White Gate VDK, for the movement of the Exim Cargo for the ships anchored in Victoria Dock. It was the same gate for which I have mentioned above for daily posting order and having Land Line Telephone.

Almost adjacent to White Gate VDK, there was Yellow Gate VDK. And nearby to it there was Yellow Gate Police Station, having jurisdiction of the docks area. The yellow gate on- duty Preventive officer used to be the nodal officer between PSO (Customs) and the police station In- charge. So there used to be lot of communication with them in case of any crime, big or small happened at the Docks Area. Occasionally petty theft cases by loaders were reported.

A little further, there was Princess Docks and Main Gate PDK for the movement of Import Export Cargo. It was very busy gate. Just outside of this gate there was Prabhu Hotel, which catered us while posted at gates. **"There were No Zomato or Swiggy that time".**

Then there was the gate called "OGPD" (Orange Gate Princess Dock") at the north- end of the Docks/PDK, only for the movements of Trailers loaded with sea containers. Customs staff going to and coming from BPT Road often used it, since it was straight and easier for car driving, instead of using the permitted adjacent yellow gate PDK, which required to take two turns. Many times, BPT and police security-Gate staff, posted at OGPD objected it and an altercation took place with the car driver. Invariably the PO posted there had to come out of the Chowki and request the security staff to allow them. Sometimes it turned out chagrined to the officer posted there.

Almost all the gates had Chakri (Pedestrian Gate) for the movements of pedestrians, mainly dock workers. These Chakris were manned by Customs Sepoys under the supervision of the respective Gate POs.

As I stated earlier, there was a functional land line at White Gate. During those days' telephones, specially having STD facility phones, were rarely available. So, we, Floating Pos, who had come from PAN India, many times tried to contact home town by dialing STD code and phone numbers just to know whether the white gate telephone had working STD Facility at that particular time and occasionally we could connect. At one occasion I also could connect to my home, but later I was told that it was not allowed and PSO can take any action. So, I wrote a note, stating the urgency to use the phone, and my willingness to pay the charges whenever asked for. Though, I did not get any demand notice from PSO.

At regular interval, floating POs were asked to report to PSO whenever they were not posted for any Gate Duty. Randomly the Escort Duties were given to "Report to PSO" officers. Escort duty meant to go along with the customs dutiable cargo from one customs-controlled area to another customs-controlled area or to some other place for specific purpose, as the cargo would not have been cleared by Customs by then. All the arrangements of transport were made by the parties, usually CHAs (Customs Hose Agents). One of the Interesting Escort Duty was to go to the office of CBFC (Central Board of Film Certification) to get the certificate after screening of the "customs non-cleared Foreign Feature Films" for their customs clearance and release in India.

During those days we were very scared of the PSO Supdts. and even did not dare to walk in front of the Batwing Swing Saloon Door of the PSO room, lest any PSO Supdt or senior PO should see our shoes from beneath the saloon door and call us for explanation that why we were loitering in front of the PSO. That was the terror in the minds of newly recruited POs. We were told that there were some supdts, in PSO who were keen observer and could identify the PO merely by seeing the shoe through the underneath open portion of the saloon door. Now I can understand that those supdt. might have acquired this quality of keen observation after working at Airport, where they minutely observed the passengers and intercepted them on suspicion for making a "Case". I can say that later I also developed a moderate sense of keen observation after doing Airport Posting and which helped me while working in AIU.

During my posting in "Floating", I gathered some more confidence having interacted with people of Pan India while performing Gate Duties. I completed my tenure in floating in due course.

Sassoon Dock: After my floating posting, I was posted at Sassoon Dock. Sassoon Dock was a place in Colaba and one of the big Fish Markets in Bombay. Duty pattern was day-night-off and Pos were posted there to Issue **"SHERA'** (शेरा). Shera was a kind of permission given In a Book (Like Bank Pass Book/Passport) to the head of a fishing boat called "Nakwa' (नाकवा,) to allow him to fish in the territorial water of India, in their fishing Trawlers, called Mothya udi (मोठ्या उड़ी, बड़ा मछुआ जहाज) and Lahan udi (छोटी मछुआ नाव) or simply Udi, usually for 15 days with the condition that within 15 days they would report to Customs on their return. Every Night different Fishermen came back, usually after 14-15 days, after doing their fishing activities, with their "Catch". I remember when I used to be drowsy in my unhygienic clumsy Customs Chowki, any "Nakwa" knocking the door coming inside and saying in Marathi "Shera dhya, Saheb., Majaha Lahan Udi Aahe" (शेरा द्या साहेब, माझा लहान उड़ी आहे... Sir, Please Give me permission, I have very small boat). The value of their "catch" could be anywhere between 1.5 lacs to 2.25 lacs in those days. These fishermen, called Kolis, were the original Mumbaikars and mainly settled in Badhwar Park, Colaba and Vasai. There were also fishermen from nearby coastal villages namely Roha, Revas, Murud Janjira, Dighi, Alibagh etc. who came to get "Shera" and for auction of their "Catch".

Then there were some evildoers, especially some of Koli Ladies, from the above said villages, who illegally brought Country made Liquor (Kachchi Daroo, ताड़ी), from their villages, clandestinely filled-in the Truck/Tempo-Tubes, in their fishing UDIs to Sassoon Dock for onward sale to the notorious dealers who later sold it to the poor addicts in entire Mumbai. Whenever they were caught, Mumbai Police was informed since it was not attracting Customs Provisions, and Police made the case.

To work in Sassoon Dock was nearly an ordeal for me. I was a Jain, a strict Vegetarian and in Sassoon Dock everywhere there was a stink of fish. There were heaps of various kind of fish which were to be auctioned/sold. On wharf and nearby approach roads, there was always slippery water dripped from the moving Tempos & hand carts, and herds of fisherman who did not take bath for months and thus emitting a bad odor all the time. For hours I had to deal with them, enquire about their catch and other relevant information to record their return and issue further "Shera" for fifteen days/One month. After working fifteen hours (6pm to 9am) in the night there, my clothes/ Uniform absorbed that fishing smell. So, whenever I returned in public transport my co-passengers looked at me with detest. Even my newly married wife used to open the door while gripping nose and directed me to Bathroom and instructed me to put the uniform and my mufti - dress in the bucket full of detergent and come out only after taking an hour-long shower.

It is not out of context to mention here that Sassoon Dock is the same place nearby Baddhwar Park/Leopold Cafe where the Pakistani terrorists "Kasab" along with other terrorists landed in a fishing Boat and who later committed the terror attack on Mumbai in 2008.

Airport: After my Sassoon Dock posting, I was posted at Airport, as Air Customs Officer (ACO) in the year 1989. The Airport Posting was mostly a time bound posting and any Mumbai Customs' PO invariably used to get it within a span of 4-5 years in normal course. The Module-2 of the International Airport, referred as "Air India Module" among Airport Staff, had just been started. Therefore, many of my batchmates had the opportunity to be posted at Airport even before completing normal four years' service in Mumbai Customs.

Airport Posting was wonderful. Meeting Hundreds of passengers, coming and going to and from every nook and corner of the world, every day and doing their customs clearance, with an authoritative attitude, was an experience which cannot be expressed in words.

I was posted in Arrival, and on the very first day At Airport, at about 2 PM I was asked to take a Red - channel counter and learn how to deal with an incoming passenger. My Counter- supdt. (Bay-Supdt.) was from Central Excise and deputed for three years under Air Pool Quota. He went up to the Conveyor Belt, just opposite to Red-Channel Counters, talked to some passengers and then brought one passenger up to my counter, inadvertently pushing the baggage trolley of the passenger.

The passenger was Pankaj Udhas, the famous Gazal Singer, and of whom I was a big Fan. So now time and again I boast that the passenger whom I cleared first at Airport was none other than Pankaj Udhas. Of course, later he became little friendly and invited me to few of his musical shows. Giving Customs Clearance as per rules, to VIP, Politicians, Film celebrities became a Norm afterwards.

In those days customs rules were very strict, (Free Allowance for incoming passengers was meagre Rs.1250/- and many other restrictions). Incoming Passengers had to spend hours together waiting for customs clearance. At "Red Channel", a written baggage - declaration was taken from the passenger, Passport was scrutinised and as per the passport details, baggages were examined either superfluously or in detail. Sometimes thorough 100 % Examination of the baggages, called RE (Re-Examination) at RE Counter, were carried out. Screening of the Baggage was mandatory. Thereafter proper duty was calculated, a DDR (Duty Deposit Receipt) was prepared for the passenger to go to any of the two

State Bank of India Counters, located behind Red Channel Counters, for paying the Duty. There also he had to stand in big queue. Only after seeing the duty paying receipt, baggage was released to the passenger by giving gate pass. Whenever any pax (passenger) was not ready to pay the Duty, a Detention Receipt was prepared, mentioning full details of the Pax, of the items for detentions and the reason for detention, and the pax along with the to-be detained package were brought to the Detention Officer (D.O.-I), who sat near the Canteen in a stinky, dimly lit room. I remember there was apparently अंग्रेज़ों के जमाने की very very heavy, might be of 150-200 Kgs, cubic shaped, 3' x 2' x 2' Iron तिजोरी, used for keeping the Punch Seals, lead seals and other important things.   To be detained packages were lead- sealed by the DO-I with the help of a sepoy and then he signed the Detention Receipt (DR) after taking possession of the package. Only after getting the signed DR, Officer and the Pax returned to the counter. So, it was very time consuming and cumbersome from the point of view of the passengers. Therefore, even big celebrities were in search of any Air customs Officer with whom they could befriended and get a little faster customs clearance on the arrival after foreign visit. Some of the film celebrities also befriended with me. One of them was GUL Anand, then a famous and renowned

Film Producer, Director who had produced good Films like Khatta Meetha, Hiro Hiralal, Jalwa, Chashme Baddoor (खट्टा मीठा, हीरो हीरालाल, जलवा, चश्मे बद्दूर) etc. After becoming a good friend of mine, many rimes he invited me to his residence for social meetings. Gul Anand resided at Prabhu Kunj (प्रभू- कुंज). The same Prabhu Kunj where the Great Lata Mangeshkar also resided. At few occasions I could also see her in person. I felt very elated after every such unexpected impromptu glimpses of a legend and almost would be on the cloud nine.

On one of the occasions, for night duty, I was posted in Green Channel, where I was to take oral declaration of the baggage items and if declared within free allowance, the passengers were directed to put their baggage on the Stainless-Steel Roller conveyor belt attached with the Screening machine, for the verification, through X-Ray images, of the contents of the baggage by the screening Officer. If the oral declaration found to be crossing the Free Allowance limit, the passenger was directed to go to any of the Red Channel for customs clearance. During the course of my duty, when there was a huge rush and big line in the green channel, I noticed one gentleman wearing three-piece suit with his wife, little nervous. I put normal questions to them with regard to their visit and baggage items, to which he replied that they were coming from Bangkok after their Honeymoon for seven days. That time Bangkok was considered a sensitive place from the point of view of gold smuggling. So, I asked them whether they were carrying any gold on their person or in their baggage and while asking I just put my hand on the arm of the gentleman. I felt that there was something hard on his arm and that it could not be mere cloth. Therefore, I took him to nearby SDO (Station Duty Officer) Room and began to interrogate him and that immediately he offered me to give something and to leave him. This was enough for me to understand that he was carrying gold. Immediately I called two male independent Panchas to witness the personal search. Also informed the Batch In-Charge, who sat on a high chair near the half circular counter of the PRO (Public Relation Officer) Customs. On personal search crude gold in the form of big "kadas" (कड़ा), were recovered

from his Arms, thighs and ankles, totally weighing around 1.3 kgs. His wife was also subjected to personal search by a lady officer in the presence of two independent lady Panchas which resulted in the recovery of around 2.4 kgs crude gold in the form of crude chains and crude gold pieces. Some were recovered from her private body parts. On further investigation one more couple who was accompanying them was also found with around 3 kg Gold. The remaining night and the next full day I was busy in completing the Case formalities. So, it was my First case at the Airport and the training given by

Supdt. Q.S. Kazi was quite helpful to complete the case formalities. Afterwards I made and participated in number of cases.

Smuggling of Gold through carriers was copious in those days. Concealing Gold in the form of Biscuits or in any other form in emergency light or other baggage items of the carriers was a favorite Modus Operandi by the gold smugglers allegedly headed by, Dawood Ibrahim. On some monetary gain Poor unemployed youths were hired to carry gold in their baggage or in their body. As Air customs officer posted in Arrival Hall, we were very attentive to the short time travelers and examined & screened their baggage thoroughly. Such short time air travelers, suspicious of being carrier, were made subjected to go through the MDF (Metal Detection Frames) to find out whether they were carrying gold on their person concealed either in their rectum or eaten, in such case the MDF gave beep Sound. Many times, MDF gave signals of metal presence on their person. After a tough questioning, carriers admitted to have gold on their person. If it were in their rectum, they were made to squat to eject the Gold. But in the cases of the gold eaten, mostly in the pieces of pea nut size, then the carriers were taken to J J Hospital for ejection of gold by administering certain medicines by the Doctors of the Hospitals. One ACO had to guard the carrier- Pax, now accused, till the ejection of the

Gold in the Hospital. So, a round the clock guarding was needed and one officer was posted for Hospital Duty to guard the accused. Every time the accused went to toilet the guarding ACO was supposed to keep an eye on him in case he ejected Gold through stool. If the gold would be ejected then count the pieces after getting these washed by the cleaning staff posted in the Hospital Toilet and then weigh it and bring safely back to the airport along with the accused. Usually, it took 3-4 days to eject all the gold pieces eaten by the accused, but in some cases, it would take even a fortnight and an ACO was invariably posted for the guard duty, who first came to Airport and only then he could know that he was posted for guard Duty at J J Hospital, (which was 30 KMs. Away from Airport), because the Posting of each ACO/ACS was known only just before the start of the shift duty. In some cases, even after the lapse of three -four months and every effort by the doctors, the eaten-up gold pieces could not be ejected, so this fact would be brought to the Quilla court Chief Metropolitan Magistrate and further action was taken as per CMM orders. Readers may well imagine the pathetic circumstances of the Hospital Guard duty.

Contrary to the deplorable Hospital Guard Duty, At Airport we had an Escort Duty, for which we had to travel in international flight, which touched enroute Indian airport as normal passenger to keep a surveillance on the movement of passengers, inside the Flight. From Mumbai Airport we escorted the international flights enroute to Delhi, Madras, Ahmedabad, Goa, Hyderabad, Calcutta, Cochin, Trivandrum, Vizag etc. on account of Air India and got very special treatment from the flight crew and pilots, who in turn also came from different parts of India. While doing Escort Duties my colleagues from different states used to bring the delicacy of that state, for example a Bengali doing escort duty for Calcutta (Now Kolkata) used to bring "Sandesh or Rossogulla" or a Hyderabadi brought "Shahi Tukda or JouZ Halwa" which we would enjoy throughout the duty hours. I ate those delicacies admiring the touch of India at Airport posting, strengthening my concept of encounter with Mini India, while working for Mumbai Customs.

In those days Air Port Posting was a Pool Posting wherein 75 % of the work strength was from Mumbai Customs and 25 % from General Pool from Central Excise. The selection of The Central Excise Officer for the 25 % quota was on Pan India Basis, hence very tough. Only competent and resourceful Cen. Ex. officer got the airport deputation posting. They were posted for three years and their cycle was made in such a way that every six months, there used to be a new lot of central Ex. Officers. And we Mumbai

Customs Officers worked with them for our entire tenure of two years.

At Airport most of the time we were given Duty in Arrival Hall For clearance of Incoming Passengers. and after an interval of every 4-5 months, we were given duty in Departure, for one month.

In Departure, every passenger was required to report to Customs Counter where our prime duties were to deter and prevent any attempt of illegal export of any contraband. Then our duties were to check the immigration Stamp on the Passport and verify whether any endorsements were there with regard to TR (Transfer of Residence) and TBRE (Tourist Baggage Re Export). Since the passenger who had availed the benefit of duty exemption of TR could not go back, for permanent settlement again, within two years of availing TR benefit. And TBRE, for the purpose of ensuring the Re- Export of the items which had been allowed duty free on his arrival after a TBRE (Tourist Baggage Re-Export) Certificate issued to him and the certificate Number mentioned on the last page of his Passport, with a direction that the Passengers would require to submit TBRE Certificate to the Officer posted in Departure and shown the items to be re-exported. In case, as ACO we found the TBRE number or TR Number on the last page of the Passport, we were to ensure that the passenger was not leaving India within two years of the TR for permanent settlement abroad and that the items mentioned in the TBRE Certificate were being actually taken back out of India.

Customs counters were behind the Immigration counters and there was appx. 150 feet gap. Passengers stood in this gap in line leaving a space of 15 feet from customs counters and one by one used to come to the counter for verification of their Passport and Boarding Pass. There used to be a long queue of the departing passengers in front of customs counters. We were required to see only passport, boarding cards and TBRE, if any, for the verification but Passengers submitted passports, boarding cards, Tickets, Invoices and many other irrelevant papers for customs. It was very inconvenient for faster verification and take a little longer than required and many time such irrelevant papers fell down and we had to bend to lift those papers. A big exercise. One of my colleagues was from Central Excise, and he used to be irritated and asked the passenger to submit only PP and BP. But invariably next passengers again submit irrelevant papers too. He used to shout **Ye Logon ko kitna bhi samjhao, lekin ye samjhtey hi nahin.** (ये लोगों को कितना भी समझाओ, लेकिन ये समझते ही नहीं, ... However hard you may try to make these people understand, but they would not understand) I used to laugh because every time there was a different passenger.

I found out the solution of the said problem. I prepared a Hand written placard bearing **Please show Only Passport and Boarding Card** and kept it on the counter and occasionally pointed out towards it to the passengers in the queue stood 15 feet away. This methodology proved effective and passengers submitted only desired documents.

I mentioned this because it carried a lesson that if you communicate thousand times with individuals it remains $1 \times 1 = 1$, and if you do not communicate individually but use advertisement methodology, communication reaches to the targeted audiences.

I often thought that I was witnessing Mini India while seeing the departing passengers in long queue in front of my counter and who came from every corner of India. And thus, that was "my encounter with Mini India" because of my service in Mumbai Customs.

Apart from duty in Arrival and Departure, we had to perform some other duties like Detention Officer Duty. There were Five Types of Detention Officers' Duty viz. DO-I, D.O.-II, DO-III, DO-IV & DO-V to keep the detained packages in safe custody. The packages could be detained for different reasons like pending payment of Customs Duty, pending adjudication, submission of mandatory certificates like Police CCS, CBFC etc. or for re-export. Detained packages were required to be routed from DO-I to

DO-V as per the reason and different stages of the detention. For example, In the cases of re-export packages, it could be routed from DO-I to DO-V till the arrangement were made for timely handing over the same to the departing passengers.

Airport was an extension of my encounter with Mini India in the Mumbai Customs. Coming across to the passengers of all parts of India, and interacting with them I understood their culture, their languages, their names, Surnames, color & creed etc. I found that by just knowing the surname one can almost get to know the state of the person, For example, Bannerji, Chatterjee, Bandyopadhyay, Sen, Sarkar etc., were invariably from Bengal, Jha, Sinha, were from Bihar, Patra, Mahapatra, Sahoo, Dash, Mohanty, Swain were from Orissa, Meena from Rajasthan, Patel, Parmar from Gujrat. Most of the male Gujrati were having BHAI and female had BEN in their names. Similarly Punjabi ladies had "Kaur" in their name. I noticed that surnames were suffixed with……. kar in Maharashtians (like Tendul"kar"). I also came to know that Hindu names were suffixed with Cristian Surnames in Karnataka and Konkan Area (For Example Rajiv D,Souza), surname ending with ...yam (like Subramaniam, Chidambaram) were from Tamilnadu whereas the surname ending with ..yan (for example Rajayyan, Rajendran) were from Kerala. Likewise Reddys were from Andhra and a south

Indian "Anna" was akin to a "Bhaiyya" of North India. Of course, this gave only a broad idea and there could be exceptions.

Facing the Bigwigs of all the states of India, watching them walking in queue with the immigrant Indian labors of middle east was just baffling and empirical. At Airport, apart from Indians of all the states, I also met the people of foreign origin like Africans, Australians, Europeans, Americans, Chinese, Thai, Japanese etc. and they also imparted little of their culture to me. Passengers from across the world going through my counter made me feel like an important person in the world, and yes, this was all because of the uniform and working with Mumbai Customs.

During my tenure at Airport, Iraq invaded Kuwait in August 1990 and Gulf War took place. It necessitated to evacuate lacs of stranded Indians from Kuwait. Air India was engaged to bring stranded Indians. Every day there were six to seven Air India Flights bringing three to four hundred expatriated Indians, mostly Labourers, in each flight, in Module-2. As per rough estimate around 170000, expatriated Indian Labourers were ferried by Air India in three months (August to October'1990) from Amman to Mumbai. The sight of those panic-stricken evacuees was saddening. Many of them were without baggage, empty handed and were not wearing even Chappals or any footwear. Needless to say that those were from

Pan India and I was interacting with them, encountering Mini-India.

In Module-1 of the Airport, a branch of the Canteen of the New Customs House was operational. The canteen catered all the officers during Lunch and Dinner Hours. It served snacks in the middle of the night at 2;00AM. Canteen Tea was always available and it could be served right on the counter, while examining the baggage. The food prepared in the canteen also represented Pan India. They prepared and served delicious South Indian snacks, like Idli Sambhar, Medu Bada Sambhar, Punjabi food Chhole -Bhature, Maharashtrian snacks Vada Pav and Puri Bhaji, Gujrati dishes Khamman Dhokla. And of course many times Bengali Sweets. During some of the night duties they served Bhajia, and Vada Pav, which we humorously called "ONGC". The Canteen boys were good and from Maharashtra, Gujrat, South India, UP, Konkan, representing many states.

Here my point is that because of this work environment, I, as a Mumbai Custom officer, all the time, encountered with MINI India.

During my Airport Posting I was blessed with a son. Gul Anand brought a beautiful Pram from London for him.

R & I (Rummaging & Intelligence): After Airport Posting I was posted in Rummaging & Intelligence. High-Profile Arora Sahab (Additional Collector Shri Laxman das Arora) was heading the R & I. He was very sharp, competent and excellent administrator and had earned a big reputation by then. He was very selective in choosing the officer to work under him in Head quarter cell of R & I. I never knew what was his criterion to choose officer to have to work under him. He had created a wonderful Network of Informers and thus many times had pin point information, mainly regarding gold smuggling, and had a large number of gold cases to his credit. However, I did not have the opportunity to work directly under him as I was posted in Adjudication Cell. In adjudication Cell I acquired good academic knowledge of the various Modus operandi used by the smugglers, applicable sections of customs act, while drafting of adjudication orders etc. which proved to be very useful in my later carrier.

IN R & I, after adjudication Cell I was posted in DIU (Dock Intelligence Unit) for a small period. In DIU there were 10-12 Officers to gather information and make cases in Docks Area. We were assigned night patrol duties also. It was in this period, to be precise on 12-03-1993, that Serial Bom Blasts in Mumbai took place. I was on day duty and getting the news of Bomb Blasts every now and then like a cricket score. "Ab Blast kahan hua." (अब ब्लास्ट कहां हुआ,) "ab kitni casualty ho gayi" (अब कितनी कैज्युअल्टी हो गई).... etc.

Later it was transpired that the RDX Used for blasts had earlier landed in a remote landing jetty at Sri Vardhan/Shekhadi, which came under the jurisdiction of M & P, a stretched arm of Mumbai preventive Commissionerate. A meeting was called upon by the than collector of customs who addressed us and explained the importance of our night patrol duty and that we were to perform our duty with utmost diligence. As DIU Officer, I took it as a challenge and did my duty with utmost care throughout my tenure in DIU. However, no case could be made, might be due to the lack of support of my senior officers who were mainly concentrating in UB Centre. UB Centre i.e., Unaccompanied Baggage Centre was meant for clearance of baggage mostly under Transfer of Residence. In the case of genuine TR, big wooden crates stuffed with all sorts of personal effects and household goods were transferred from the foreign country by the transferee and required to be examined thoroughly as there was concessional Customs Duty or no Duty on used items under TR with some conditions & restrictions. But in reality, there were many Non-genuine TR Goods from Dubai or other Gulf Countries and the big-big wooden crates flown from these places contained all types of commercial and dutiable goods mainly electronic goods, cutlery items, crockery and many other high valued items and possibly concealed contraband and restricted items. Wooden crates containing such commercial items instead of genuine personal effects and house old goods were called **"CITRA"** (सिट्रा) and were subjected to 100 % examination. I could smell that some of our senior officers knowingly cleared them not following the due diligence. After clearance these commercial goods straight away transported to "Musafir – Khana" which was a hub of imported goods for retail selling. Needless to say, that I was mainly doing my duty in other parts of the Docks and rarely came to UB Centre, since I was too junior to question my then seniors who, as DIU Officers, were ignoring the clearance of such CITRA packages, and which were cleared by uniformed- examining- preventive staff. Sometimes later CBI entered in UB Centre and halted the clearance of CITRA.

While doing one night duty I received a phone call from Arora Sahab to accompany him up to Santacruz AirPort, as he was leaving for Allahabad on transfer.... At Santacruz Airport he talked about intelligence work, cultivation of informers, my experience & working in R & I and what not, while standing and sipping coffee at the Tea-coffee shop counter. It was my last meeting with the high-profile customs' additional Collector. After few months, might be due to the alleged enmity, while working with Mumbai

Customs, germinated between him and the dreaded smugglers, on 24 March 1993....

he was assassinated in Allahabad.

Wadala Incinerator Plot (WIP): After R & I, I was posted at various Bunder Postings like Haji Bunder, Hay Bunder, Wadala Incinerator Plot, (WIP) Lakri Bunder etc. The Wadala Incinerator Posting was very convenient to me since I was staying in Five Gardens Customs Colony which was hardly 3 kilometers away. WIP posting was 24 x7 x 365 on Day-Night-Off pattern and three POs were posted for doing shift duties. So, I had the duty on Sundays and on another Holidays also on my turn, though there was hardly any work or movement in WIP on these holidays. So, on those holidays I used to take my son, who was around 5-6 years old, with me on my Bajaj Scooter to WIP, for time pass. Me, my son and one of my sepoys used to play cricket in an empty 40' container, lying opposite customs chowki Thus me and my son liked the WIP Posting very much.

Lakri Bunder: Contrary to WIP Posting, my posting at Lakri Bunder was "a whole different ball of wax". Lakri Bunder posting was also round the clock gate posting. We were three POs to do the preventive duty in shifts i.e. Day -Night-Off. Basically, in those days, Lakri Bunder was being used for bringing and unloading the Sea-Sand (Reti). So, all the time Wharf was wet, Muddy and dirty. Our duty was to take frequent rounds of the wharf and nearby areas to prevent mainly any unauthorized landing of smuggled goods, which could be even gold, Silver or restricted & prohibited items from Dubai or Pakistan. Those days this landing route was supposedly in use by the smugglers, in light of the RDX landing at Sri Vardhan. Which was used in the Serial Bomb Blasts in 1993. Therefore, we had to be extremely alert and take frequent rounds. Our Chowki was very shabby and dirty. There was not regular cleaning in the absence of regular janitorial staff. There was a Junked cycle in the Chowki, earlier given by the depatt. To take rounds. It was regularly mentioned in the asset register, and we had to "receive and hand over" the junked cycle at the time of start and end of our duty timing. Since it was junked, flat tyres, inoperable handle, and without seat, we could not use it. So, we had to walk down in the entire dirty area. Taking preventive rounds in the night was horrible. There was no Light, so we had to carry Torch in our hand in that slippery, filthy wharf. Adding insult to injury was that the area was full of stray Dogs, who always barked at us while taking rounds and we had to run to keep our body parts intact. Few hundred meters away, there was a ship wreckage yard also, where small vessels were dismantled from time to time. So, whenever such vessel arrived for razing, we had to walk down up to that area, chased by the barking dogs. Mere remembrance of those rounds gives me goosebumps even today. Somehow, I completed my tenure diligently.

The purpose of mentioning the above narrative is to high light the totally different work environment in Mumbai Customs. At one hand there was Airport Posting at the clean and posh Airport and on the other Hand at Lakri Bunder.

Airport: In 1998, I was again posted at Airport And a fresh cycle of interaction with the passengers Pan India and from all the five continents started.

In my second Airport postings, I met with the same duty responsibilities which I have mentioned in my earlier Airport Posting, though I found lot of changes in the procedure of customs clearance, which was the after effect of the opening up of the Indian economy led by Shri Man Mohan Singhji through his 1991 landmark Budget, influenced by the worldwide policies of "Glasnost & Perestroika". The import of Gold was allowed on payment of duty in foreign currency on completing certain conditions. Free Allowance which was earlier mere 1250 was raised to Rs. 12000/- per passenger. The overall effect of the less stringent customs rules was that less crowd in arrival Halls and fast clearance of incoming air passengers. Oral declaration of the baggage given by the passengers were accepted in normal course, thus creating a faith on each other i.e., between customs law enforcing officer and the passenger.

During my second Airport stint also apart from general passengers, NRIs, I had the opportunity to meet a number of VVIPs, film celebrities, Politicians, Industrialists, Renowned Doctors, Scientists, other Professionals etc. I also happened to befriended with Dr Nitin Dhedia, who was the first Eye Surgeon of Mumbai, who had specialised in Lasik surgery. I used to wear specs from my school days, so when he convinced me about the safety, I went ahead for Lasik Surgery as advised by him and thus got rid of spectacles.

All the narrative mentioned in my first Airport posting can be reproduced for my second stint at airport. During my second stint at Mumbai Airport, as usual I was also given Departure Hall duty. In the day time there were very few flights and departure hall remained almost empty in day time specially after noon. Only the passengers of one or two flights were to be attended for departure clearance. My son was now 8-9 years old and, on few occasions, I took him with me for day duty, as the security was not strict during those days and many of our officers brought their kids while coming on duty specially in Departure. I showed to my son what to verify and how to verify the passport and how to put Customs Clearance Stamp on the Boarding Card giving practical lesson. Watching this some Passengers used to be very happy and loved him saying CHHOTA

Customs Officer. Now those are happy memories and my son also remembers the Mini India characteristic of Mumbai Customs.

As per the policy I was also posted for six months in the prosecution cell. Prosecution cell posting meant to attend the CMM court or High Court of Mumbai in pursuance of the smuggling cases made at Airport. For the purpose I had to brief our council so that he could represent the department effectively in the court. Many times, Judge/CMM also put direct questions to the attending officers. So, I had to be well versed with the facts of each and every case and the Laws applicable to. Attending the drugs cases was very terrifying since the judge asked difficult questions as the severe punishment was depending on the merit of the case beyond any doubt. Our councils were Advocate Mr. Arun Gupte, Advocate Mr. Inamdar, advocate Mr. George, Advocate Mr. Natarajan. All were experienced but Mr. Arun Gupte was first among equals. In most of the cases defence councils were Mr. Rizwan Merchant and Associates, Mr. Kantawala, and in few cases Mr. Majeed Memon. I must say that all were eminent and efficient lawyers of that time. My prosecution tenure was very hectic but I completed it very satisfactorily.

After prosecution posting, I again posted in Arrival and departure duties periodically and did normal airport duties.

On 26 January 2001 an earthquake of extreme intensity jolted the Kutchh region of Gujrat. It killed around 20,000 of people and destroyed lacs of buildings. There were many Gujrati NRIs from the reason. They were panic-stricken and worried about their relatives in the quake affected area. So many Gujrati NRIs came to India (Mumbai Airport) to see their relatives and friends in the Kutchh Region. I was interacting with them and clearly could read Anxiety, distress, fear and trauma on their faces. Many were telling the unpredictability of life. As normally Indians talk in such situation. My encounter with My Mini-India.

Air Intelligence Unit: Thereafter I was posted in AIU. Working in AIU at Mumbai Airport was one of the best customs duties in Mumbai Customs, provided an officer was willing worker and created the work for himself. AIU posting was on the pattern of Day-Night-Off- Off and of 12 hours. The work load in the day duty was not much since the number of Flights were less. But Night Duties were very hectic. Those days around 150 flights were operated and as intelligence officers we had to scrutinize their IGMs/EGMs and chalk out our course of action to make a case. Entire Airport, be it Arrival Halls of both the Modules, Departure Hall of both the Modules, Tarmac, Transit Lounge, Airlines counters etc. were our fields for intercepting passengers. We were a team of sincere

IOs and made a number of cases especially gold cases.

In AIU my Batch worked very hard day and night and made many cases. We had to walk around 10 Kms In night duties. We had to run from Arrival Hall Module -1 to Arrival-Hall Module-2, Both the Modules' Departure Halls, Transit Lounge, Tarmac, etc. as per the arrival and departure of flights specially flights coming from and going to sensitive places like Dubai, Sharjah, Muscat, Bangkok, for gold smuggling and Nairobi, Addis Ababa, Dar es salam etc. for narcotics Drugs to intercept the doubtful passengers and make case.

During my tenure in AIU, we made many cases and noticed novel Modus Operandi to smuggle gold and drugs. We found out that crude Gold in the wired form could be conceal in the specially made grooves of a trolley bag or suitcase, Crude gold could be conceal in electric motors of Mixer-grinders, gold biscuit could be concealed in the nappy of a toddler in hand, it could be concealed in children toys, concealment of gold after wrapping with carbon papers, it could be brought on person, Gold could be handed over to the Airlines Staff for taking out of the Airport, Gold could be left in the Aircraft, to be collected later by cleaning staff of the airlines, gold biscuits could be handed over to tainted immigration officers in the Cigarette packet while getting immigration clearance, Gold could be smuggled with the connivance of hands in gloves Customs Officers, uniformed as well as AIU Officers . Similarly Foreign Currency could be exported illegally concealed in clothes, on person, in vegetables, in Mangoes after removing pulp & Seed and then stuffing FC wrapped in cello Tape etc. Similarly, Drug could be concealed in the False Bottoms of Suitcases, in the guise of medicines, in the food containers, in the hard cover page of a book, in the hollow rods of trolley bags etc. I must say that smugglers were very innovative in evolving methods for smuggling activities. In this connection once I was told by an accused of gold smuggling that in Dubai there are jewellery shops which could supply the crude gold in any form/in any shape as per the order of anyone and that Gold Smuggling was in total control of notorious gangster Dawood Ibrahim. As I mentioned in the narrative of my first Airport Posting, still the Gold was occasionally smuggled in eaten pieces by unemployed youths, called carrier, on the payment of some money.

There were four Batches of AIU, called Batch "A", Batch "B", Batch "C" and Batch "D". Every Batch was given a trained Canine with an experienced Dog Handler. These dogs created a fear in the passengers specially Africans and helped in detecting narcotic drugs and thus making a drug case. The name of One of the Canine was "Hero". And it was really a Hero since it detected many Narcotics items, cleverly concealed in the baggages of drug smugglers.

Whenever we made cases, it required photos to be taken for the purposes of evidence, press, other batches, or for our personal record. Since the cases could be made at any time, two photographers were always available and who were given requisite permissions to work at Airports. Their names were Sharmaji and Khatri. In many cases they were made panchas also. Besides, whenever any VIP or Film celebrity came to Airport, they were always available for ACOs and ACSs for the photo – shoot along with the celebrities. Readers may recall that by that time Smart Mobile Phones had not come in the hands of people, so selfies could not be taken.

Similarly, there was one Pot-bellied Patiram who ran a restaurant in Transit Lounge and was always available with his KHICHDA, whenever batch officers felt hungry, during the process of completing case formalities, at odd hours like 5, O'clock in the morning or six O'clock in the evening.

During that time Amitabh Bachchan's TV show Kaun Banega Carorepati (KBC) had just started and all of our officers were much fond of the programme and were impressed a lot. So as per my suggestion we started our Batch's own such general knowledge programme in the name and style of "**Kaun Banega**

Dau Sau Pati" (कौन बनेगा दो सो पति,). Every Officer rotationally set the questions at home and brought it to office and during our Lunch/Dinner, we tested our General Knowledge, Numbers were given on the basis of right answers by the question Paper setter officer and the winner used to get Rs. 200, collected from all the participating officers.

I enjoyed the AIU Posting a lot in true sense. The experience I got in AIU cannot be expressed in words. I can say that it was the best period of my career in Mumbai Customs. Needless to say, that AIU posting strengthened my notion of paradigm shift of Mumbai Customs to Mini India as I was posted in AIU only because I was the part of Mumbai Customs.

Manufacturing Bond: After AIU, I was posted in a Manufacturing Bonded Warehouse, Effusive Enterprises, located at MIDC Khairane. It was managed by a Lady, Smt. Veena Punjwani, who was very competent. She reminded me the women-force of India. Again, encounter with mini-India. In the manufacturing bond, I had the opportunity to watch the manufacturing process of tooth Brushes. I intensified my knowledge of export procedure from the point of view of an exporter, which helped me in doing my duties in the docks and export sheds.

Nhava Sheva (JNCH Port): In the year 2002, I was Posted at Nhava Sheva Port as PO, by Mumbai Customs being the Cadre Controlling Authority. That time Nhava Sheva Customs was functioning from the old barrack type office premises, which was a very small place considering the work load and so-many customs sections/cells. The Building of JNCH was nearing completion and the process of shifting from old Barrack building to New Seven storied, consisting three wings, of beautiful Jawaharlal Nehru Customs House (JNCH) had started. Initially I was posted in floating to man the gate duties. As far as I remember that time there were only six gates on which floating Pos were posted to supervise the movement of cargo and pedestrians. The gate duty at Nhava Sheva Port was not as strenuous as it was at Mumbai Docks' Gates. There was not surprise night visits of superintendent, as almost all the superintendents resided in Mumbai suburbs roughly 60 kilometers away.

I being a reluctant daily traveler took an accommodation at JNPT Residential Colony. So doing my floating duty was not much difficult for me.

Meanwhile on 23-09-2002 I was promoted as Superintendent of Customs (P). and posted in Nhava Sheva R & I Section. In Nhava Sheva R & I by then not separate cells had been formed as Mumbai Customs' R & I like Head quarter, Town notified area,

Investigation, adjudication, prosecution etc. since there had been minimal work and as such there was not much backlog of cases to be handled. I remember doing some odd work of intermingled sections/cells. My main work was to assist and supervise the shifting of old records, Files, furniture etc. to New Building. New building of JNCH was very specious for the then posted customs staff who were operating from the small barrack. So many rooms were on our disposal and officers were free to choose any room from the available rooms as per their liking. No set norms were finalized wrt to section wise occupation of the office rooms. I remember the pleasure of selecting one or two rooms for a section from available so many rooms.

Here I would like to mention one incidence which had been empirical for me. On one fine day, when I was busy in the record shifting work from Barrack type Customs Office to the Newly Constructed JNCH, I was presented with an opportunity to take a Helicopter ride as an escort Officer, without any hesitation and any other thought I agreed for the same. The helicopter belonged to one Mr. Schmitz, a dashing German National who was on his world exploration tour on his personal 2-seater Helicopter. Mr. Schmitz had rough-and-ready knowledge of English Language.

Mr. Schmitz was on his adventure of world tour on his personal Helicopter but due to some technical reason he had to ship his chopper in a Sea shipping container from middle east to Nhava Sheva Port, and Mr. Schmitz himself later came by air at Mumbai airport. On being informed by the shipping line that his Chopper had come to Nhava Sheva Port he came to Nhava Sheva Customs House (JNCH) for the clearance of the Helicopter. Though Mr. Schmitz was not acquainted of the procedure, still he had not engaged any handling customs House Agent and was running here and there in the JNCH for the customs clearance. Since the Helicopter had been imported in a sea container, it could not be cleared without paying customs duty or otherwise as per the rules and only after completion of certain formalities. Finally, he could meet the then ACPG (Assistant Commissioner of Customs, Preventive General). After understanding the full case and formalities to be done it was decided by the ACPG that the Helicopter would be escorted by some experienced/senior Officer up to Mumbai Airport and who should ensure that it leaves Indian Territory. However, due to long distance back from Mumbai airport to Nhava Sheva, and considering it as an unprecedented escort duty none of the floating escort officers was willing to take up the opportunity. So, when I, being a recently promoted superintendent from Senior Preventive Officer, was asked to do the escort duty, without any hesitation and for the excitement of getting a ride in a personal 2-seater helicopter, I willingly nodded. So, I was deputed to escort the two-seater Helicopter. Thereafter, I, along with Mr. Schmitz reached to the Nhava Sheva Docks area, where the Helicopter was lying in one 40' container, with blades detached. The Helicopter and Its blades were destuffed from the container and thereafter the blades were Re- fixed with the help of some port workers. After hours of Labor-intensive work by the port workers the chopper was ready to roll. At around 6:30 pm Mr. Schmitz sat on the pilot seat and I on the adjacent co-pilot seat in the Helicopter, to escort the helicopter from Nhava Sheva Port to Sahar International Airport, Mumbai. My very first experience of such a grunting machine, and before I could understand or ask anything we were already hovering near and above Mumbai airport. It took just 12 minutes to reach the Mumbai Airport. A road journey which would have taken about 2.5 hrs. via road was completed in mere 12 minutes. But then the helicopter had to hover in the air for more than 20 minutes at the Mumbai Airport since the permission to land was not given by the ATC because it was not scheduled flight and No flight plan was submitted in advance as per the rule. Meanwhile the fuel gauge was almost on red and speeding to "E", I saw Mr. Schmitz restlessly talking to ATC. Apparently, he had become very impatient. Noticing this, I asked Mr. Schmitz to hand over the headset to me so that I could talk to the Air Traffic Controller. I explained the situation to the ATC in Hindi after giving my identity and requested him to permit us to land as soon as possible. Then only ATC gave the permission to land and a remote Bay was allotted to land and park the Helicopter. Once the Chopper parked, Mr. Schmitz was eager to fill up the Chopper fuel tank, but he was not knowing anyone or the procedure. So, I had to take the situation in my hand to help the gentleman. Fortunately, I knew some of the Airline people, since I had recently worked at Airport. I somehow contacted them on the tarmac, while they were doing their duty in the airline vehicles, which were having passes to run the vehicle on tarmac. Ultimately after having exchanged few words, I was able to arrange fuel for the Chopper for which Mr. Schmitz paid the Bill in USD. By than it was 10:30 pm. Still my escort duty was not over as the helicopter was still not customs cleared and it was very much in Indian Territory. Mr. Schmitz just bewilderedly looked at me. It was the situation where I was to take the decision. So, I brought Mr. Schmitz, taking a lift in one of the Airline vehicles, to the Assistant Commissioner of Customs, Airport, who, was sitting in the Arrival Hall of module-1 terminal building and who was the jurisdictional in charge for the night. I explained the entire situation to the AC. He was very cooperative and allowed me to go to ATC Tower for the purpose of Flight Plan submission. This was something exceptional considering the strict security norms. The AC, Airport also provided me his official car to go to the ATC. Even in ATC Tower, it was not easy for me and Mr. Schmitz to meet the Air Traffic Controller. After a lengthy argument with the security staff there, we were able to meet ATC on duty. Again, I had to explain him the entire situation. After a few ifs and buts he agreed to accept the flight plan and asked Mr. Schmitz to submit the same. That time Information Technology was not so advance what it is now and Mr. Schmitz was not having his laptop with him. So, Mr. Schmitz sat there in the cabin of the ATC and prepared the Flight plan and submitted the same to the ATC. Now, there was further problem. There was not an available slot in which the Helicopter could fly from the airport since it was very busy night at airport and many scheduled flights were queued up. Anyway, after taking into account of all the flights, ATC gave the time slot of 4:30 am-5:00am. Now still matter was not ended. Now the question arose of customs clearance, submission of EGM. So, we again came to the Terminal Building and met the Superintendent in charge of Field Security who was also handling the charge of Non-Scheduled flights. He noted down the details and advised us to submit EGM to Departure Superintendent. Accordingly, we came to the departure area which was at first floor, crossing many security hurdles. There Mr. Schmitz prepared a hand written EGM and submitted it to the Departure

Customs. After scrutiny of the same Customs Clearance was given. But that was not the end of the ordeal. Now question arose of Immigration Clearance. Again, I had to come forward for the help of Mr. Schmitz. I took him to the Airport Departure Immigration Officer on Duty. Again, explained him the entire episode. The Immigration Officer verified the passport of Mr. Schmitz, Obviously the Passport had the Arrival Stamp of the Immigration which was put at the time of Mr. Schmitz' arrival at Mumbai Airport. Thus Mr. Schmitz was given Immigration Clearance. Now the problem was how Mr. Schmitz would go to the place where the Helicopter was parked, since it was at a faraway Bay. I again came forward for his rescue and took him to the parked helicopter, in the Official Car earlier provided by the Airport AC.

Finally Completing the set of formalities, and all set to take off, we took a sigh of relief, Mr. Schmitz was very much relived and he thanked me a lot. He said "he could not imagine that an Indian Customs Officer would help him so much out of the way and that he would remember the incidence and me for long" We Shook hands and I bade him farewell and wished him Bon Voyage for his remaining world tour. He sat on his Pilot seat and the gigantic blades of the Helicopter started rotating and few minute later Mr. Schmitz was gone. I saw the Helicopter, which I had escorted from Nhava Sheva Port, disappearing into the vastness of the sky for leaving the Indian Territory. For an escort duty, which I had thought would take a mere 30 mins, turned out to be a nightmarish of 12 hrs. escort duty.

On completion of my R & I tenure in Nhava Sheva, I was posted at CFS Maersk as export examination Supdt…. Readers may recall that I had mentioned, supra, that Appraising wing handled the examination of Import export cargo at the time of my joining in Mumbai Customs. The then strength of both the working Appraisers and the Supdts. was sufficient for handling the work load. Later it so happened that at one hand work load of examination of Exim cargo kept on increasing and on the other hand number of appraisers diminishing due to their speedy promotions and no fresh recruitments. So, it was decided by higher authorities to give Exim cargo examination to Supdts. also. As a result of this policy change, we Supdts. of Customs were gradually posted for cargo examination.

While working as export examination Supdt., I gained the knowledge of the various items being exported from India. I noticed that brassware & Handicrafts were mainly manufactured and exported from western UP, Buffalo leather & Pan Masala from central UP, Food grain from Punjab and Haryana, Hosiery items & sports goods from Ludhiana, Tirupur was a major textile and knit wear hub contributing to 90% of total cotton knit wear exports from India, Three-wheeler Autos, engineering and medicines from Pune, Clothes from Surat Gujrat, Buffalo meat and fish from Maharashtra, Stones from Rajasthan. Ceramic Tiles from Morbi Gujrat, etc...

Thus, readers may notice that I was continuously encountering mini-India while working in Nhava Sheva Port which was under the administrative control of Mumbai Customs.

MMTC: After completion of my Nhava Sheva tenure, I was posted in P & E Section for a very short period and then on my request deputed at MMTC Strong Room at Air Cargo Complex as assistant Custodian. As I wanted to do a correspondence course of "Post Graduate Diploma in Human Rights" from IIHR New Delhi, I requested for deputation in MMTC Strong Room since it was considered a leisure posting. MMTC Strong Room posting was 24 x 7 x 365 posting manned by three Pos. So, I had to do night duties there also. Here there was a little work in day Time but night duties were very busy. In fact, MMTC Strong Room was a Transit Warehouse, where precious and semi-precious cargo like Diamond, emerald, Sapphires, Ruby ,Gold jewelry studded with these stones were kept for safe custody in case of Imported Cargo after receiving them from various flights (through the escorting POs posted in ACC

Batch) and till their dispatch to Bharat Diamond Bourse (BDB) Offices at Opera House and in case of to be exported cargo after receiving them from Opera House till handing over to the escorting Pos who were to hand over the same to captain of the concerned flights. There used to be on an average 700-800 small - small sealed packets in any night duty. The value of these packets could be anywhere between 300 crores to 500 Crores. As Asstt. Custodian, I was responsible for their safe custody, and to check the seal intact and maintain their records. Hence all the time every pore of my body had to be alert. To render logistic support to Assistant Custodians, BDB had provided very sincere and experienced support staff. After sometime, I realized that they were quite reliable. Not a single untoward incident happened during my tenure.

During my tenure in MMTC there had been the much talked about torrential rain in Mumbai which resulted deluge on 26th July 2005. By chance, I was on Off Duty, but the other Asstt. Custodian having previous night-duty had a very tough time for two days.

Since during day time there was not much work, I could prepare for my PG Diploma on Human Rights as envisaged by me before making the request for deputation for one year which was extended for further one year as per my second request.

I passed the Exam of PGDHR with distinction.

Airport: After completion of my deputation in MMTC, I was posted at Airport for the third time. During this tenure I found lot of changes due to the economic boom.

I was posted in Arrival Hall. That time Sudts. were doing baggage screening at green channel. Since I had some experience of Screening of baggage and detection of contrabands and dutiable items, because of my earlier working in AIU, almost routinely I was given screening duty and I can say that I justified my posing at baggage screening Machine and detected many contrabands and restricted items and diverted the passengers to red channel for appropriate action. Stainless Steel Roller conveyor belts were attached with the Screening machine, one carrying the baggage inside the machine and the other for carrying the baggage out of the machine. The ball bearings of the Steel Rollers were worn out and made Ear piercing, loud hoarse noise. Since I was regularly posted on the screening machine for almost five months, this exposure of raucous earsplitting noise affected my ears adversely. On my regular yearly medical checkup, it was diagnosed that I had started developing SNHL (Sensorineural Hearing Loss) coupled with conductive hearing loss. It was very disheartening to know that there was no medical cure for the hearing loss and I had to live with the hearing loss and only Hearing Aids could give me some help. So, I had to use Hearing Aids, which I am still using and waiting for some miracle cure of my SNHL.

As per the policy of six months posting, I was posted as Supdt. Main Warehouse. Main warehouse was a big warehouse in the Module-1 of the Airport near the customs canteen and a cashier's cabin. Main warehouse posting carried a big responsibility of safe custody of more than three thousand detained packages, waiting for clearance as per rules or disposal. Packages were kept on the slotted angle storage racks of changeable heights. Everyday there were lot of incoming and outgoing packages, of which I had to make entries in the Register. Deep inside the main warehouse there was a Strong Room wherein gold and high value packages were kept in iron Pigeonhole Almirahs under the charge of Strong Room Supdt. Who sealed the strong room with a temper proof lead seal. There was not much regular work for the strong room supdt. At the time of going off duty I also had to Seal the warehouse very carefully. In the duty time my movements were restricted even for going to toilet, because of security reasons. Apart from this there was a big problem of Rats gnawing of the packages. So, I had to procure rat poison and mousetraps to keep away the rats from the warehouse, Since I would have been answerable in case of any damage to the passengers' baggage.

To reduce the problems, in consonance of the Strong Room Supdt. I found out one solution. I occupied the cash cabin, which had been then vacated by the cashier. I operated from the cabin for the purpose of making register entries and keeping the packages for temporary safe custody. I opened the warehouse for a limited period, whenever necessity arose. Thus, I had some peace of mind in warehouse posting, which otherwise considered a difficult posting. Here I would like to mention that passengers wanting the delivery of their packages, which had earlier been deposited with (DO-1) (detention Officer) and from whom the packages were received in the main warehouse were from pan India, thus giving me some experience then and there of Mini India.

After Main Warehouse posting I was regularly posted in Departure for few months on my request (because of hearing problem). I found a lot of changes in Departure working. The scrutiny of Passports was discontinued as the endorsements wrt TR (Transfer of Residence) & TBRE (Tourists Baggage Re-Export) were no longer been made due to the orders by competent authorities as Passport was considered Personal Property of the Pax and so it could not be used as Customs record paper. Departure staff was posted mainly for issuing export certificate, maintaining per Capita Register (Detailing the Flights data) and selecting 7-8 % suspicious passengers at random from the passengers list given by the airlines, and question them with regard to contents in their baggage and on person, whenever they reported. In the night times there were big queues in front of many Immigration Counters which were placed in front of the Customs' single Departure Counter. There were two Big Screen TVs were installed overhead between Immigration and customs.

On one of the occasions, I found Sunil Gavaskar standing below one of the TV Screen in a long queue of passengers mainly consisting of gulf laborers as two three Gulf Sector Flights were in the process of departing. His surrounding persons in queue were tall and well built within whom he looked a little fragile frame. And then there was an advertisement on the TV Screen just above the Sunil Gavaskar in which he himself, Sunil Gavaskar, was shown in close ups and in a big Frame. I was startled seeing the coincidence of the real life and the reel life.

Similarly on one of the occasions, I had a chance to meet Mr. Resul Pookutty. He had just won the Academy Award (Oscar) for Best Sound Mixing for the film "Slumdog Millionaire" and was coming from America and going to Trivandrum in connecting domestic flight. So, he had come to my counter to submit the mandatory declaration of Domestic Passengers. He had mentioned about the Trophy in his declaration. He was carrying a normal Shoulder Bag. But It was not an ordinary Shoulder Bag. It contained the Pride of India of those days. I requested Mr. Pookutty to show the award Trophy, which he gladly did. I was ecstatic on touching the Oscar Statuette.

During my entire tenure at Airport, there had been regular interaction with the passengers belonging to all the parts of India, and because of my default inquisitiveness I learnt almost all the aspects of Indianness, which ultimately, again, strengthened my concept of lexicalizing Mumbai Customs as Mini India.

Air Cargo Complex (ACC): Thereafter I was posted in Air Cargo Complex for two years. My second time ACC posting was given to me after 22years. Initially I was posted for Air India Spare Bonded warehouse. This warehouse was meant for storing Aircraft spare parts, which were imported by Air India and on which no customs duty was paid. These were issued whenever needed for repair of the Air India Air Crafts. I saw and gained knowledge of the different air craft parts from entire engine to a small nut-bolt. These were delivered in the hangars. Though I had not had an engineering back ground still I was fascinated by watching the repair of Aircrafts. I used to put some preliminary questions to Aircraft Engineers and got satisfactory answers. Needless to say, that the Engineers were hired from all of India and I saw the mini-India in them too. After Air India spares Bond, I was posted for EGM reconciliation Cell. There was a huge pendency of EGM Error because of which Drawback could not be disbursed to the exporters. There was a big pressure to release the drawback so that there could be more liquidity in the hands of the exporters and thus ameliorate exports. I thoroughly understood the problem of generation of EGM Error, understood the Customs EDI Menu which could remove the EGM Error if certain data were fed in the System. I repeatedly followed up the exporters on line and got the details required to enter in the EDI System. Thus, A substantial pendency was reduced to the bare minimum level. My bosses were very happy and other Customs Commissionerate were flabbergasted for the ACC Customs Commissionerate's speedy reduction of EGM Error pendency. Since the Commissionerate wise Pendency reflected on customs portal and some of them contacted my AC to know the method of reducing the EGM Error. I explained to them in the politest way. Thus, again coming into contact with the people pan India.

My next local posting in the ACC (Cargo) was examination of export cargo. As I said earlier because of increasing workload export examination had been given to preventive supdts. There was a tremendous work load of examination of Export Cargo IN ACC. That time there used to be on average of 2000 S/Bills, (Shipping Bills-Export Consignment) per day which were to be handled by Eight Supdts in two shifts, morning and Afternoon Shift. Morning shift was 8 am to 4 pm and Afternoon Shift 3pm to 11pm with one hour overlapping for handing over and taking over. In the morning shift work would be started actually after 10 am but we had to attend at 8 am in the case of any urgency emerged. There could be any chartered Cargo flight to upload the cargo any time in the morning and the customs clearance was a must for the same. Cargo Fights or Chartered Freighters could not be delayed. On an average 250 S/bills would be handled by each Supdt. In a duty of eight hours a supdt. was to verify the Inspector's examination report, inspect and examine 100 % of the packages, selected by the ICES, which could be anywhere between 10-12 for a consignment of 150 to 250 packages. This required to go into the export shed from the cabin, roughly 100-meters walk, get the packages opened, examine and repack into our presence as any of the consignments of the 250 S/Bills could be used to conceal the contraband, then come back and feed the report in the ICES, generate LEO (Let Export Order) and sign the physical copy of the LEO whenever presented later by the party/agent. If the examination were conducted as per the rules, in its strictest sense, only 50 S/Bills could be handled. But we had to handle 250 S/Bills otherwise export would have been affected. And this was every day's affair. And because of lack of the availability of required strength of Supdt., more supdts. could not be posted for the same. Now the readers may consider the workload and the responsibility attached with it. Here we had to depend on our past experience and thorough scrutiny of the documents. Fortunately, nothing untoward happened in my tenure.

Here I would like to mention one incidence. There was a pregnant cat, who roamed in the Export Shed and official cabins installed therein. People working there gave some foods to her. One fine day, I was having Morning shift duty and had reached to my Cabin exactly at 8 am. Only to find that the cat, now not appeared expecting. Obviously, she had delivered kittens the previous night, and now was rambling in my cabin.in search of food. As it is well known that after the birthing process of the last kitten, cats feel terribly hungry and require plenty of food. Before I could arrange some food for her, suddenly the Cat pooped, in the shape of a round cake on one of the office tables. Hunger is a primal animal urge that drives them to find, acquire and consume whatever is within their sight. So, the cat once looked this side and then on the other side and just started gobbling its own poop due to the hunger and not availability of any other food in her sight. I was just stunned watching the Cat, devouring its own poop. Inadvertently it reminded me the stories I was told in my childhood about the famine of Bengal in1942, when starving people had to eat the flesh of their own dead children to satiate their hunger....

Many readers may find it not worth mentioning, but it was a startling sight for me that time and for a long time I was engrossed in the thought of pangs of hunger.

After Export examination, I was posted for Batch duty wherein I was to do the examination of perishable cargo in APEDA (Agricultural and Processed Food Products Export Development Authority) Shed to give the LEO (Let Export Order) for same, Give direct delivery of the goods of time bound clearance like lifesaving medicines, Flowers, and other highly perishable cargo, News Papers, Magazines. It was of the pattern of Day-Night-Off and having 10-12 officers in each batch....

While performing my duty I came to know that highest qualities of Mangoes were being exported to Gulf Countries, specially to Saudi Arabia. The importers at SA were very strict about the quality of Mangoes and literally believed in the proverb of "One Rotten Mango can spoil the entire basket". So even one or two mangoes in a lot of 100 boxes contained bad or rotten Mango, they did not accept the entire lot and could withhold the payment. So Indian Mango Exporters were very careful and could not afford to delay the shipment in time and for which they arranged the chartered cargo freighters. While working in APEDA I also came to know that mainly Alphonso (Hapus) and other types Mangoes like Dashahari, Kesar, Gola, Langda, and Grapes, Pomegranates, Naseberry (Chikoo) Chilies, Gingers, Onions, Leafy vegetables were exported. I think this may be one of the reasons of high prices in the domestic market of these agriculture products. But the export was also necessary to earn the Foreign Currency for the economic welfare of our country. Thus, I also came to know which crop produced in which part of India. Like I came to know that Alphonso was mainly produced in Ratnagiri & Deogarh, Valsad and south Gujrat, Grapes in Nashik, Sangli, Satara & Ahmednagar, Pomegranates in Solapur, Chikoo in Navsari & Valsad, Chilly in Guntur, AP, Lasalgaon in Nashik is the main distributing center for Onions, Ginger is mainly produced in Madhya Pradesh. I also came to know that Sea Foods like, Pomfrets, Shrimps, and other fish were also exported from the coastal area Konkan and Maharashtra on regular basis.

So, I encountered mini-India in Mumbai Customs 'controlled Air Cargo Complex Postings too.

Nhava-Sheva (JNCH): After my second ACC posting I was again posted at Nhava-Sheva (JNCH) for second time. By this time, I had become senior Superintendent. Nhava Sheva port had also been widened with three terminals (JNPT, NSICT & GTI) and which had crossed 32 million TEUs with its stretched arms of about 28 CFS (Container Freight Stations). Now it was the biggest port in India in terms of containerized cargo Handling. Initially I was posted for examination of export cargo and issuing LEOs. The details of the same I have mentioned supra so I would not like to repeat the same. The other postings I was given in Nhava Sheva (JNPT) port are mentioned hereunder:

MTO: After export Shed, I was posted as MTO (Motor Transport Officer) JNCH. This was a posting of big responsibility. All matters related to departmental Vehicles, (Cars, Busses, SUVs) and the vehicles provided by CFS (Cars), were required to be wielded by the MTO. There were many issues like which boss wanted which particular type of vehicle, along with which driver. Timely attendance and availability of the of the driver, breaking down of the car during journey, Traffic violation by the drivers etc. For any mistake of the driver, MTO was held responsible. ("One incidence I also faced when the wife of a very seniormost Officer assigned the job to the Driver to take the dog outside for poo and come back before the Sahab gets ready to start for the office. The dog did not poo for a long time. The fearful driver phoned me, and asked me what to do" ... Ludicrous isn't it.!) Then there was the necessity of timely maintenance and servicing of cars, keeping the log books, a tedious procedure of condemnation of old vehicles etc. During my tenure one problem of payment to the Bus contractor "Bothelo" also arose. Three busses were hired from Bothelo for the use of Appx. 150-200 Staff members who resided in Dadar, Andheri and Thane and its nearby areas. The distance was appx. 60 kMs. and it took 2-2 1/2 hours as the road condition was not good. Also, there was no good and speedy direct public transport. The payment to the contractor Bothelo was being made from the welfare fund from the CBEC board. It so happened that for five months payment could not be made as it was not received from the fund from Delhi. After three months Bothelo started pressing hard for the payment. I had brought the issue time to time into the knowledge of the higher bosses who always instructed me to persuade the Contractor Bothelo to wait for the payment. I somehow cajoled Bothelo to continue with their service, but after fifth month, they gave ultimatum to discontinue the bus service, since they were unable to bear the cost of Diesel and salary of the their drivers. Discontinuance of bus service meant that 150-200 staff members either coming late in the office, facing the hardship of public transport or in worst case remain absent. I conveyed about the ultimatum of discontinuance of busses and explained the gravity of the matter to the higher bosses. After a long discussion I was directed to go to Delhi personally by any flight in emergency and bring the Cheque for the payment to Bothelo. I was given assurance that the Air Fare would be reimbursed to me. Accordingly, I went to Board Office in Delhi and met all the very- very senior officers, including Member administration and even to the minister of state of Finance and briefed them the issue. And regularly giving update to the higher bosses in JNPT. Eventually, within two days I got the cheque issued for the payment to Bothelo.

It is pertinent to mention here that I was not reimbursed the Air Fare because I had not gone to Delhi by Air India Flight.

That time MTO was also holding the charge of group D staff (Havaldars, Sepoys, Loaders) This was also equally tedious. Preparing their monthly posting, keeping in view of their old postings and that which boss wanted which sepoy for his office work. That time all the serving Havaldars/ sepoys/Loaders were locally recruited from the lot of land owners, whose ancestral lands were acquired by the Govt. for developing the Nhava Sheva Port. So they were very stubborn and sometimes did not obey because of their unity. To keep them under control was really challenging.

Boarding Office: After MTO Posting I was posted for Boarding Office. As boarding supdt. I boarded the incoming vessels along with my subordinate boarding team. Took rounds the ships, checked their bonded stores, examined the IGM. And other related documents as per the rules. There were many vessels on which Indian Crew were there. These crew members belonged to different parts of India and as such while interacting with them, I felt the aroma of the whole of India. Whenever we worked for long hours, and at Lunch times, we were offered lunch by the captain of the Ship. Many a times I refused, since being a strict vegetarian, and thought that non-Veg oil (Like cod liver oil) was used in preparing the food. However, whenever convinced that the food was strictly vegetarian, I had the lunch offered to me. This way I learnt about and tasted the veg'-continental food, Thai Food and veg Mexican food.

Export examination: After my Boarding posting, I was due for Import examination being a very senior supdt. By then, but instead I was repeated for Export Examination. Obviously Import examination was demand posting and I was a **"Square peg in a round hole"**. In export examination I did the same duty which I have mentioned at some places above.

SIIB (X): After completion of my Nhava Sheva tenure, I was posted in SIIB (Special Investigation and Intelligence Branch) (Export). Here there was lot of file work. I had to go through the old cases files, did follow- up actions wherever needed. On going through the old cases, I came to know that in one case, even the extended period of five years under the section 28 of Customs Act-62 (applicable in the cases of suppression of facts), was going to be over within three weeks. I immediately brought the fact into the notice of my the then Deputy Commissioner who instructed me to prepare the Show Cause Notice as soon as possible. Accordingly, I worked on the SCN even in the late nights, all seven days, forgetting any holiday and thus was able to complete a flawless draft SCN well before one week of the dead line of issuing the SCN. It was presented before the then Commsissioner, Export. She went through it thoroughly and appreciated my effort of completing the flawless draft SCN of demanding customs Duty of more than 74 lacs, that too within a short time.

My posting in SIIB Export had been ephemeral for me as during this posting on 22-10-2014 I got promotion as Assistant Commissioner of Central Excise and Customs along with my Batchmates vide a general promotion order No. 192/2014 of CBEC Dated 22-10-2014. In pursuant of the order, I was relieved on 10-11-2014 to join in Vadodara Central

Excise Zone. I received the relieving Order with a mixed feelings of Joy of promotion and a heavy heart of leaving Mumbai Customs.

And thus, my long-lived affiliation with Mumbai Customs, specific epithet in this book as My Mini-Inia, ended, leaving everlasting memories.

MY Colleagues in Mumbai Customs Mini India

In my early days as an employee of the Bank, I had come in contact mainly with localities, i.e., Rajasthani and other Marwaris who later I figured out were orthodox in their thoughts and I rarely came across persons from different ethnic background. The whole scenario had changed for me once I joined Mumbai customs and started working in New Customs House. Our Seniors then, were mostly Maharashtrians, South Indians Anglo Indians, etc. The specialty of these people was, that they were very clear in their conversation, "calm and collected" and spoke without hesitation, with some exceptions. Perhaps this is the reason they were very confident about the post they held and always commanded respect and position they were in. Those worthy senior officers were the ones who taught me how to command attention and respect. How to make sure, that the common man takes a note of the uniform and not the man inside it irrespective of caste, creed or religion they belong to. My colleagues were of all different background, I had Maharashtrians, Gujaratis, Haryanvi, Biharis, UPites (Who were colloquially called Bhayyans) Odians, Kannadigas, Punjabis, Delhiites, Catholics, Andhraites, Bengalis and others from almost all parts and places of India. This is where I learnt that Mumbai Customs is not less than Mini India.

I joined "Our Mumbai Customs" in 1986, it meant that the Customs Act-62 had been enforced just 24 years before that and the many officers recruited after the implementation of CA -62 were on the verge of retirement (That time retirement Age was 58 years) So I had the opportunity to be guided by those experienced officers. Among those was the last and old lot of Anglo-Indian Officers, who were recruited through Employment Exchange. Their names were enough to scare a junior novice officer like me…. Kingsford, Providence, Hancock, Julian, D mellow, to name some of them as I had not come across many Anglo-Indian persons at my native place. Today I may say that they might not be knowing legalese minutiae of the Customs Act, except chapter XIII, but they knew very well how to command the respect from the public and juniors.

At the time of my joining Mumbai Customs in 1986, the total strength of preventive cadre was Appx. 3000 (Supdts, POs. and Sepoys- Havildars) Out of this 3000, appx. 600 POs. were recruited directly PAN India, through SSC. The direct recruitment for PO had started from 1978 through SSC. Prior to 1978

POs. were recruited locally through Employment Exchange. Apart from the academic qualification, one of the criteria was the bodily fitness of the candidates. And therefore, I found that the Officers recruited through Employment exchange locally had a well built and good height. Many of them were Six footers and had dominating personality as customs officer. Bombay being itself a cosmopolitan City, the local recruitment also represented by the officers belonging to different parts of India. Moreover, Then Collectors posted from IRS cadre. Hence, they were also coming to Bombay representing different Parts of India. For local recruitment of POs. they were the appointing authority. It reflected in their selection of POs also for example during the time of a South Indian Collector many south Indian persons were recruited as POs. What I want to Highlight is the fact that even before the direct pan India recruitment of POs, the preventive cadre was having officers from different part of India. After 1978 direct recruitment PAN India strengthened the Mini-India shape of the Mumbai Customs.

As I said earlier my colleagues belonged to different states. In fact, they were from each and every State of India. one may name any State and we had the officer of that state. This is why I have kept the heading of this book as **"My encounter with Mini India in Mumbai Customs"**. Officers belonging to different states as my colleagues meant that they were teaching me indirectly their culture, dressing clothing, food, languages, rituals, festivals, eating preferences, habits, vices, way of treating people etc. for example I learnt that Lord Jagannath is the most revered Deity for Odians, Maa kali, Durga Maa for Bengalis, Tirupati for Tamilians & Andhraites, Sabrimalai for malyalis, Maa Ambe or Ambaji for Gujratis, Ganpati,/ Vinayak/ Bappa, Vithoba & Mahalaxmi for Maharashtrians, Maa Vindya Vasini, Mayyhar Devi for MPians, Khatu Shyamji & Savalia Baba for non-Jain Rajasthanis, and Chhat Maiya for Biharis etc., I tried to learn the basis of their faith and many of them explained it to my satisfaction.

I learnt that Bengalis liked Machh Bhat, Fish Fry and preferred Hilsa Fish while Maharashtrians liked Pomfret (paaplet), Bombil, Bangda, Rawas and Surmai etc., I found Konkani & Goans were more interested in Lobsters and Shrimps in the category of non-Veg Sea foods. Whereas Punjabis, Haryanvi, Bihari were more interested in chicken and mutton and were less tend to like sea foods, whereas Odians liked both. I, being a vegetarian could never try any of these but have always heard my other colleagues talk highly about their preferences and preparation of the dishes.

I found that Gujratis, Rajasthani, have smaller percentage of non-veg eaters and that Keralite like coconut preparations more and like to eat on banana leaves. UPites and Biharis would often bring Home made Sweets, or from an expensive Mishtan Bhandar, I always found, those sweets had a different flavor and taste.

When I was posted at Air Cargo first time, in 1986 one of my colleagues "Soni" once brought a bucket full of Undyo, a Gujrati delicacy, and all the colleagues enjoyed the Undyo with Bread slices full night. Undyo...! I heard and tasted first time. Some of my Keralite colleagues brought Puttu, a Keralite delicacy, which also I heard and tasted first time. Some of my Sindhi Colleagues from Ulhasnagar brought Daal-Pakwan and "Gayer" a different version of combination of Rajasthani "PHEENI and GHEWAR". Some of my Odian batchmates brought "Khaja" and "UKHUDA" from Puri after visiting Jagannath Yatra. On one occasion I, myself, took Rajasthani delicacy Daal-Bati and my colleagues enjoyed it.

Notwithstanding having different delicacies, preparation and taste, most of my colleagues and batchmates unanimously liked i.e., Drinking Alcohol and smoking. Boozing during any party was as essential as staple food. There were very few colleagues who did not drink and smoke. Initially I was a teetotaller, but later became a social drinker for not to be isolated in a social gathering. Though, I never smoked. For me, to adapt the taste, Spice,

Sweetness, oiliness, dryness, drinking etc. was a whole different kind of pan India experience. Which in my own thinking, I would not have had in such a short period, had I not been in Mumbai Customs. So, this was not just Mumbai Customs for me, but it was India within 4 walls of New Customs House. Soon enough the vast experience I got felt equally grand as of the magnificent New customs House.

I found my south Indian colleagues celebrating Onam, Ugadi, Pongal. Punjabi Friends celebrated Guru Parb, Vaisakhi Lohiri with great Zeal and all the officers of other states too celebrating with them in Customs Colonies. Similarly, the craze of Gujrati Folk dances Dandiya & Garba, during Navratri in customs colonies was eye-catching. Bengalis were delighted during Dashara time doing Kaali Maa/ Maa Durga Puja in big Pandals. Maharashtrians celebrating Ganpati Bappa Maurya during the 11 days' celebration of Ganpati-Pooja & Visarjan. My Maharashtrian colleagues consecrated Lord Ganesha Idol at their homes and invited other colleagues to have Darshan and Prasada. My Odian Colleagues always tried to take leaves to celebrate Jagannath Rath Yatra in Puri and talked a lot about the experience they had during the Yatra. Likewise, some of my UPite colleagues went to attend the Nauchandi Mela in Meerut. My Punjabi colleagues went to Amritsar to visit Harmandir Sahib Shrine/Golden Temple, whenever had the opportunity. Visiting Shirdi Sai Baba often, was a norm for all my colleagues irrespective of their connection of any particular state or religion. Maharashtrian colleagues often went for Ashth - Vinayak Yatra, Bhima Shankar and Mahalaxmi Mandir at Kolhapur. My Keralite friends went to Sabrimalai temple and even after coming back, wore black cloths for further few days Many of My Muslim colleagues went for Haj in Saudi Arabia and Khwaza Moinuddin Chisti Dargah in Ajmer, and also visited locally Haji Ali Dargah, Haji Malang or Baba Makhdoom Dargah or to Minara Masjid, My Christian friends went to Mahim Church, Victoria Church. They invariably attended the annual fare organized at Mount Mary Church at Bandra and shared their experiences with rest of the colleagues. Once in a year, "Satyanarayn-Chi-Maha- Pooja" was organised by preventive Sepoys-Havildars at the ground Floor Conference Hall New Customs House, which was visited by the entire Customs Staff including the Bosses and Apprasing wing Officers, who represented the whole of India. Thus, I always found engulfed in the Mini-Indianness of Mumbai Customs as far as religion was concerned too.

I found my Punjabi & Haryanvi batchmates often giving audacious remarks but at the end of the day they proved to be very helpful, caring and clear-hearted and "Jindadil" people. I found, Andhraites,

Kannadigas and Konkani people most sophisticated, balanced, indulgent and soft-spoken people. I noticed that Maharashtrians displayed different gestures while speaking to Maharashtrians and all together a different gesture while speaking to non-Maharashtrians in a natural way. Rajasthani colleagues always gave Marwari tone while speaking. I noticed my Odian & Bengali batchmates good Hindi Speaking people but not so good in reading and writing and many times perturbed with lesser used Hindi words. One of my senior officers was from Jammu & Kashmir and spoke equally good Urdu and Hindi. My Himachali friends always talked about beauty of Himalayan Range/peaks and about the young people of their state who preferred to join defence services, in good Hindi. My UPites colleagues often talked about the sanctity of Banaras. I found some of my Bihari batchmates always trying to dominate others by way of ridiculing them. Also they talked about the old heritage of their state and importance of Patna Sahib and Chhat- Puja in their life, in teachable Hindi.

I did not find much difference in clothing as ours was uniformed service, and normal attire was pant & shirt. Most of us usually kept shirt in, whereas the old Maharashtrian colleagues found comfort in Out Shirt. Occasionally and on some festival celebration I found many of them wearing Kurta Payjama, Some of My

Muslim friends came wearing Pathani Suit and Skull Cap during the festival of EID. My south Indian colleagues specially came wearing Mundu after the celebration of Pongal and Onam. Keralite friends came in Black Dhoti Shirt after visiting Sabrimalai. Many of my colleagues came tonsured after visiting Tirupati.

I found Muslim officers going to offer Namaj every Friday afternoon and no boss ever denied permission to them for the same. All officers enjoyed Holi, Diwali together, Local Maharashtrians and Mumbaikars enjoyed Gudi Padwa, Bhai Beej, freely after adjusting their duties with non-Maharashtrians The same way Christians and Maharashtrian officers went Wednesday Mass Prayer at Mahim Church a little earlier. New Year Eve Celebration was waited for eagerly right from the conveying good wishes on Christmas by all the Officers. I found Jain and Buddhist officers were minimal in the Mumbai Customs, hence, their festivals were not conspicuously celebrated, except the gazetted holidays on Mahavir Jayanti and Budha Jayanti.

Some of my Maharashtrian colleagues flew Kites on the occasion of Makar Sankranti at Nariman Point or Juhu/Mahim Chowpatty. Gujrati colleagues went to Ahmedabad for Kite flying and after return, talked a lot about the kite flying Zeal in Ahmedabad. I myself had been a good Kite-Flier, since Kite Flying is also celebrated with great enjoyment & Fun in Rajasthan so I could feel their enthusiasm.

Some of my colleagues were Hockey players who had represented India in Olympic games also. I found them, very practical and dashing with a very Happy go Lucky attitude. Few of them were made protocol officers and PROs and they were quite successful in their assigned duties. One was Mr. I S Grewal about whom I have mentioned in my ACC posting. Then there was Mr. Mir Ranjan Negi, the famous or infamous Hockey Goal keeper on whose life the Film "Chak De India" (in which Shah Rukh Khan acted as protagonist), was made. He was a party freak and very candid to me, as he was to everyone, and whenever we met he invariably and smilingly asked, "Aap ke Balon ka raj kya hai..?" (आप के बालों का राज क्या है ...? What is the secret of your hair.?), since I had long hair.

Some of my colleagues were Cricket Players who represented at State level and were good friends of legendry Cricketer Sachin Tendulkar and Vinod Kambli. So many times, when Customs Day or any other event were celebrated by Mumbai Customs, they were invited and they attended the functions gleefully. On certain occasion Tendulkar himself came to New Customs House for meeting the Chief Commissioner for his Customs friends.

There were Some Lady colleagues. Majority of them were Maharashtrians. Almost all of them were replica of Indian Women as generally perceived. They wore Sari, Bindi, Bangles, some facial make-up and ornaments. Some of them even wear Festoon (Gajra) as headdress on festivals. I found them very soft spoken and kind hearted as expected from ladies. In my opinion they were giving good impression of India to International passengers at the Airport. Two of my such Colleagues were Mrs. Gaikwad & Mrs. Dalvi, who resembled one of my elder cousins, were very cordial and on few occasions, we visited each other's home and familiarised. Some of my Lady Colleagues were Christians, south Indians, Sindhi & Gujrati. I found them rendering good official duties in normal course. But one thing was there, all lady officers were always ready to work in night duties only at the Airport and not at any other places giving this reason or that reason. Administration also considered their requests favourably many times.

Some of my senior colleagues were related to each other. For example, there were Patel Brothers, Mansharamani Brothers. In one case there were four members of a single Maharashtrian Family in Mumbai Customs. Then there were cases of Husband and wife working together in Mumbai Customs. In one case one of my junior colleagues had almost deserted his wife and having affair with another female colleague.

There were cases of relatives in Havaldars and Sepoys also. I write this only to highlight that even on social front Mumbai Customs was representing Mini-India

My colleagues, senior or junior, whenever they met after sometimes always started with "where are you posted now...?" "पोस्टिंग कहाँ पर है ? Invariably the main purpose was to know about the posting at "Sensitive" or "Non- sensitive" category. Then they talked about the posting in great length, about the pros and cons of that posting and that how differently they were handling the said posting then others. At the end no one was happy with his posting whether it was sensitive or non-sensitive.

Today, when I regurgitate, I deduce that generally the behaviour of the majority of my colleagues in Mumbai Customs had been professionally appropriate. I was given full cooperation and moral support by them in general and by senior Mohammedan Colleagues in particular in the initial years of my service. Yet, there were some senior colleagues who were not cooperative and tried to create hurdles for me in discharging my duties efficiently. Some of my own batchmates were following the aphorism **"jo kaam kare usko ungli karo, phir Boss se uski chugli karo"** (जो काम करे उसको उंगली करो, फिर बास से उसकी चुगली करो.. **First Irritate the**

person who works and then do backbiting to the Boss). I know some of my own Batchmates, who traduced about me on my back many times to my immediate bosses and because of them I got a Bad APAR/ ACR (Annual Performance Appraisal Report/ Annual Confidential Report) and thus did not get fair posting in Nhava Sheva. God Bless all of them.

During the initial years of my service, I also realised that there were many groups of officers bound by some common factors like:

Sportsmen-Group, Sindhis-group, Muslims-group, Christians-group, south Indians-group, Maharashtrians-group, Haryanvi-Punjabis-group, Bengalis-group, Odians-group, Biharis-UPIites-group, Rajasthani- Meenas Group, Ulhasnagar-Officers-Group, Malad-Borivali Officers Group, Kalyan-Dombivali Officers Group etc. And then there were some non-group offices like me, a Rajashani-jain, who were not fitting in any group. Since there was not any common factor, which was necessary for inclusion or formation of a group and not being in sufficient number. I do not say that this groupism was harming the official duties in any way, except in few cases of favoured postings. These groups were formed just for the convenience and improving social relations among them. This groupism was mainly noticed while the members of that particular group used to be involved in conversation. For example, a

Sindhi Officer talked in Sindhi Language while speaking to other Sindhi Officers. Similarly, a Bengali in Bengali language and Odian in Odian language, so on and so forth. In many cases an Officers used to be the member of another group and followed the same pattern like Ulhasnagar- Sindhi Officer speaking in Marathi while speaking into a Maharashtrian group. And a South Indian speaking Hindi while talking to a Upite.

Mumbai Customs also had some officers whose integrity was doubtful. I could smell that some were indulged in nefarious activities. In our indicative parlance, they were doing Fix-o-Fix for "Kudkum (KK)" at Airport. Some were definitely hands in gloves with duty evaders and smugglers, at ports & other places. Many of them had hired private boys to collect their graft. Few of them were caught time to time. Whenever there was anticipation of raid by any outside agency like DRI or CBI, a phrase "Garam Hawa" (गरम हवा) could be heard in the entire office premises. Mumbai Customs also could did not remain untouched with the forgery by the officers as few of the Preventive Officers were removed from the service because they had submitted Forged Sports person's certificate. This is now open secret that In India, some sections of people are getting recruited in government offices on the basis of forged certificates. This requires to be thoroughly probed.

Changes/No changes I witnessed

During my career in Mumbai Customs, I witnessed it functioning under 20 different Principal Collectors / Chief Commissioner/Pr. Chief Commissioner. They all were brilliant, visionary, respect commanding and good administrators who brought requisite changes in Mumbai Customs to make it the best Customs Commissionerate in entire India and making it replica of Mini India.

When I joined in Mumbai Customs in 1986 there had been one customs Collectorate for handling entire customs business in Mumbai and its vicinity, One Collectorate of Airport including ACC and one Preventive Collectorate. Steadily manifold increase in customs work, and to handle this greater work load efficiently, necessitated to create New Customs Commissionerates. Hence Mumbai Customs Collectorate was carved and restructured and with effect from November 2002 three Customs Zones came into existence. These three Zones now have multiple Customs Commissionerates. Strength of

Preventive staff increased so was senior Group A officers of customs posted in Mumbai.

Now there are 20 Customs Commissionerates in three Mumbai Customs Zones. Viz. Mumbai Customs Zone-I, Mumbai Customs Zone-II and Mumbai Customs Zone-III.

Under the jurisdiction of Mumbai Customs Zone-I, there are Six Commissionerates (One General, Two Import Commissionerates, One Export Commissionerate, One Appeals Commissionerate and One Audit Commissionerate. (Pr) Chief Commissioner Mumbai Customs Zone- I, is the Cadre Controlling Authority of the Preventive Cadre. Under the jurisdiction of Mumbai Customs Zone-II – there are seven Customs Commissionerates (One General, Four for IMPORTs & Exports, One Appeals and One Audit Commissionerate. Under the jurisdiction of Mumbai Customs Zone-III there are seven Customs Commissionerates (One General, One Airport, One Import, One Export, One Airport Special Cargo (APSC, for Precious Cargo Customs Clearance Centre (PCCCC), Airport Sorting Office (APSO) and Courier Cell) One Appeal (ASC) and one Preventive Commissionerate. The Strength of Preventive staff also increased along with the senior Group A officers of customs posted in Mumbai. However, the Cadre Controlling Authority for the preventive cadre is still

Mumbai Customs Zone-1, keeping its Mini India character intact.

When I joined Mumbai Customs, Mumbai Docks had Nine gates (Detailed in my Floating Posting Above) for the movement of Import Export cargo and "Chakris" for pedestrians. These gates were manned round the clock and around 54-55 Pos were posted in floating to man these gates. Gradually the number of gates were reduced due to their less requirement because the containerised cargo movement was picking up rapidly. The quantum of Import Export cargo had increased manifold, for which these gates were found incompatible and as such the Docks were reshaped. There were Huge-huge warehouse Sheds in the Docks and in the vicinity to keep Breakbulk Cargo for safe custody. After my joining in 1986, since the mode of transportation of import export cargo from breakbulk was rapidly changing to containerized cargo in 20' and 40' containers. So, there was a rapid decrease in the utilization of warehouse sheds. I witnessed slowly- slowly sheds were disappearing and the movement of Container Trailers increasing in the docks and on roads. The ratio between breakbulk cargo and containerized cargo was 8:2 which now has been changed to 1 : 9

When I joined, the port of Nhava Sheva (Jawahar Lal Nehru Port) was under construction and it was under the jurisdiction of Collector Mumbai Customs.

Now it is a full-fledged separate Customs Zone i.e. Mumbai Customs Zone- II. When I first posted at Nhava Sheva, a barrack was the work place for Customs. And PUB (Port Users Building) for other port agencies. Then considering the work load to be handled by the Nhava Sheva Port in future, the construction of big Customs House opposite the barrack was planned. The construction of Jawaharlal Nehru Customs House was completed in front of my eyes. On 14-08-2003 it became operational. JNCH is a beautiful seven storied building and having three wings. I witnessed the shifting of the Customs office from the Barrack to the JNCH.

Similarly at the Sahar International Airport, I also witnessed the construction and revamping of the then both the International Terminals viz. Module-1 and Module II of the Airport. Earlier there was only one Terminal for all the International Flights. Due to the increased in the Passengers traffic, Module-II had been constructed. This also necessitated the increase in the strength of ACOs and ACS. Flights' operations were segregated as per the Airlines. Module- I was earmarked for other airlines' flights and Module--II was meant for Air India. There were only 14 Aerobridges-Gates. Surprisingly there was not gate 13, as it was considered inauspicious. Earlier Collector of Customs (Commissioner of Customs) Airport used to sit at first floor at arrival hall of Module-I. In 2010 the same was shifted to Avas Corporate point, Andheri East, a place roughly two kilometres away from CSMI Airport, Mumbai. Now there is complete renovation of the Airport and I find it difficult to associate myself with the new Airport building since I did not work here as customs officer.

There used to be an almost empty BPT Road, where I could drive my scooter from five Gardens, Wadala to Greengate/Customs House in almost a straight line without any traffic signal at the stretch of 14 kilometers in the heart of Mumbai. Now there is zigzag road full of vehicular traffic and having overhead Metro line. I saw the coming up of a Ganpati Temple on this road just before Yellow and Orange Gate. I witnessed it becoming big to bigger.

Mumbai Customs Officers' Residential Colony at Five Gardens has been revamped. One of the Five Gardens opposite the South Facing Gate of the Colony used to be grassy and we sat there on the Side Benches. Now the Garden is no grassy anymore and has become sandy and used by the youngsters to play cricket and Football.

As the shortage of residential Official quarters was being felt continuously, another big "Customs Colony at Powai, Andheri", and A 20 + storied sky scraper called "Lloyds Estate Customs Quarters, Wadala", consisting of two wings was got Constructed and acquired. Now Mumbai Customs Officers of all Ranks are allotted Quarters in these colonies, somewhat relieving from the shortage of Official quarters for Mumbai Customs Officers. Mumbai Customs Officers, who hail from almost every part of India, celebrate all their festivals zeal fully in Customs Colonies. Thus, resembling Mumbai Customs to Mini India.

A plot of Land measuring 55 Acres, called "Suleiman Shah Compound", was there in the name of Salt Commissioner at Wadala. In late nineties, after all out efforts by the then CHS Supdts. duly guided by the higher ups, the same was taken over and unsocial elements who had encroached over there were removed. Now the planned construction of a big Complex of Customs Offices, & various Directorates, thereon is underway. After its completion Mumbai Customs would have better infrastructure to perform.

There had been a spree of changing Names. Bombay became Mumbai by a legislation in 1995. So many entities containing Bombay in their names had to resort to substitution of Mumbai for Bombay like Bombay Port Trust now known as MbPT. However, some establishment did not change their name like Bombay Hospital is still Bombay Hospital. IATA Code is still BOM. Though the name of Sahar International Airport Bombay changed to Chhatrapati Shivaji International Airport Mumbai in 1999 (Maharaj was inserted in 2018. In line of changing the names, I also changed my name from Hemendra Kumar Jain to

Hemesh Chhabra in the year 2000. The reason for changing my name was not social or political like Bombay to Mumbai but was Cheiro's Numerology.

During the opening up of Indian economy pursuant to "Perestroika and Glasnost", it was felt that the word collector sounded coercive and needed to be changed. Earlier class one (This description of Class -I Officer itself changed in 2015 as Group A Officer) officers of Customs were called as Collector (With prefix as per the hierarchy like assistant, and Deputy) Therefore, vide The Gazette of India extraordinary dated 27-05-1995 the nomenclature was changed from collector to Commissioner. Further new designations felt to be created to differentiate the seniority of Group A officers. and as on today the designation are Assistant Commissioner of Customs, Deputy Commissioner of Customs, Joint Commissioner of Customs, Additional Commissioner of Customs, Commissioner of Customs, Principal Commissioner of Customs, Chief Commissioner of Customs Principal Chief Commissioner of Customs. All these senior officers of customs are posted in Mumbai Customs as per the rotation Policy of the Board (CBEC, now CBIC). These officers also enhance the Mini India characteristic of the Mumbai Customs.

When I joined the retirement age of Central Government Employees was 58 Years. In May' 1998 it was increased to 60 years. Our very senior colleagues Like Shri T. Jayaraman, T.V Shankar and others who were pulling their socks up to get retirement, were suddenly informed that they were not going to be retired for further 2 years and thus were pleasantly surprised. We were also happy to be benefitted with their guidance and experience.

Some other changes which I witnessed, were gradual and keeping the pace with rest of India, due to the revolution of Information Technology. Earlier Shipping Bills and Bills of Entry were prepared manually by the exporters/Importers or their CHAs and submitted to Customs. This was stepwise step replaced by the filing of Electronic S/Bills/ Bills of Entries, after the launch of ICES (The Indian Customs EDI Systems), which was a flagship application of NIC, and launched in the year 1995. It was the outcome of a systems study conducted by NIC & CBEC (National Informatics Centre and Central Board of Excise and Customs (Now CBIC), from the year 1992. Now almost all the documents like Invoices, Purchase Orders, Phytosanitary certificates, fumigation certificates, Certificates from CITES (Convention on International Trade in Endangered Species of wild fauna and flora.) wherever necessary, EGMs (Export General Manifests), IGMs (Import General Manifests), etc. can be filed electronically and thus, removing a lot of paper work. Introduction of E-office has almost detracted the Physical- Nadewala-

Red Flap files from the Office Tables. Similarly, In the early years of my service in Mumbai Customs, I had to stand in the Queue opposite Cash counter at third floor of NCH, to collect my monthly salary. But lately, salary was credited directly into my bank account.

I witnessed the revamping of Customs Guest House at the third floor of New Customs House. Now it is one of the most exquisite Customs Guest Houses in all over the country. Likewise, Earlier The departmental Cars used by higher ranked officers having red bacon on its roof were invariably Ambassadors. Now other Cars like Innova or Scorpion or other Hybrid cars without bacon but with white curtains are being used by the Commissioners and above. I also witnessed the departmental Cars being replaced by the Hired Cars/vehicles, and the behavioural change of the Drivers.

The changes which I have mentioned above were adopted to keep a pace with the changes made throughout India hence, the Mumbai Customs also showed its characteristic, discussed herein, of being Mini India.

Some changes which I witnessed as Mumbai Customs officer may not be treated as worth mentioning by others but I do notice the same in the back of mind. Like, The Musambi-Orange, Pineapple Juice- Wala is not present now at the outside of the functional main vehicular gate of the customs House, who always poured some more juice in your glass after you finish the ordered one glass of Juice, with a smile on his face, that smiling face is not there now. Similarly other eating stalls have disappeared. All the eateries, and other roadside Bakhdas were run by the people who had come from the different parts of India. Talking to them, interacting with them, put them together gave me the flavour of Mini India while working in Mumbai Customs. However, even after 37 years I do not find any substantial change in New Customs House. The building is almost same except few renovations without any structural change. Control Room is in the same room. Backside south-eastern Gate is still dysfunctional. Canteen is at the same place at ground level, though a major revamping done up. Head of the Mumbai Customs (Now Principal Chief Commissioner of customs) still sits in the elegant chamber at second floor. Though the number of the names of the persons who held the post, mentioned on the display boards which are embedded on the side wall of the chamber, have increased. The laboratory is still at the same floor, oozing out the chemical smell all the time. The rush of the customs house agents is the same who are always in a hurry. The Abu Moosa Shop from where I got my first uniform and other customs accoutrements is still there on Walchand Hirachand Marg, though the Red Gate Opposite it, is disappeared now.

The paper Wala displaying daily newspapers and Customs related Books on the road outside the Entry gate of Annex Building, is still very much present. The banana Wala still serving bananas at the same place. Bombay Coffee House is same, even though the change of Bombay to Mumbai did not make it Mumbai Coffee House. National Hindu Hotel is same where I along with my colleagues used to go to have a byte during Lunch Hours. Hotel Prabhu, outside the main Gate, from where we got our food served while working gate duties is still very much present there. Young boys still play cricket on the Roads, adjacent to Customs House, on Sundays and other Holidays.

Epilogue

It consumed 28 years of my youth and middle age working with Mumbai Customs in NCH, till I was promoted in Group A service in 2014. Now I am a retired Asst. Commissioner. I have the leisure to evaluate my association with Mumbai Customs. I can say that not a single day had passed by wherein I had not learnt something new about our people in India while working with Mumbai customs. In my 28 years long journey, I had met with, worked with, interacted with, partied- hearty with, disagreed with, spent time with people almost from every corner of India. Understood their culture, their behavior, their line of thinking, their ways of communication. I tasted their delicacies, enjoyed and participated in their functions and festivals. Understood their rituals, their Faiths, their prayers, things they do in certain situations, their clothing, and a lot more. Though a lot has changed in this period specially because of revolution in Information Technology. Official physical files are replaced by e-files. Official Communication from hard copies to soft copies, emails. Letter replaced with phone calls, and phone calls became a text msg on mobile so on and so forth.

But certain things still remain the same way in Mumbai Customs. Officers employed in Mumbai Customs still give it the colour of Mini India. Bengali Officers still love Maach- Bhaat, and are Fine Art Lovers, Gujrati Officers still go crazy over Undyo, Dhokla, Khakhra & Dandiya & Garba Dance during Navratri. Punjabis still are the high spirited (Pun intended) Jindadil customs officers, Maharashtrian Officers are still broad minded but reserve for non-Maharashtrians. UPites colloquially called Bhayyans and Biharis are still loquacious Officers. Kannadigas and Konkani still are soft spoken. Rajasthani, usually referred as Marwaris are still misers, Haryanvi and Delhiites are still boasting but helpful. South Indians & Konkanis are still balanced and having scientific temperament. Odian Officers are still tolerant people. What I want to say that whatever I learnt about India and the basic nature of Indian folks during those 28 years with Mumbai Customs, is still relevant. and therefore, I can dutifully assert **MY ENCOUNTER OF MINI INDIA IN MUMBAI CUSTOMS.**

Customs Department is wrongly believed to be a corrupt department in general and Mumbai Customs in particular. But Corruption is individual's choice and it cannot be associated with any particular government establishment as a whole. Every Government Servant is fallible to corruption. Corruption is present in every Government department with a difference of degree. Corruption is built-in human character by nature. It runs in the veins and hence it infects everyone, lesser or more. In my early days in Mumbai customs my senior officers would often tell me ..''Don't **run after money and money will come to you, if it is there in your destiny. Bhgya mein Paisa hai to aayega hi aur Bhagya mein nahi hai to aakar bhi chala jayega.'** (भाग्य में पैसा है तो आयेगा ही, और भाग्य में नहीं है तो आकर भी चला जायेगा), I remembered their "Mantra" throughout my service-career and today I can proudly boast that because of this "Mantra", I had peace of mind and could complete my entire service career without any blot or blame of corruption.

I have given the details of my Posting History for the main purpose to familiarize the readers of various places, nature & conditions wherein a preventive officer of Mumbai Customs had to perform his duties, and of course, through this way I could revisit my journey in Mumbai Customs. My effort may also enable my the then colleagues and the persons connected with Mumbai Customs during the period of 1986 to 2014 to recall their experiences. I have taken care of full diligence while narrating my posting history, however, It is an span of more than 36 years and I have been dependent entirely on my memory so inadvertently some deviation of the facts might have occurred, which, if any, I am ready to accept and expect from esteemed readers, my colleagues, and other confederates to please ignore.

I have mentioned few names in this book in good faith and without any malafide intention, whatsoever, and which surreptitiously crept into my mind, as a flashback, while writing this book. As such I expect it would be welcomed wholeheartedly by them and their acquaintances in good spirit.

I have also mentioned few of the instances as per my own point of view. Not necessarily that others may have the same view because of their own experience. Some of my Batchmates, my colleagues may not be in consonance with my narrative in this book. It is quite natural and expected because everyone has different perception in a given situation as per his enculturation. However, if there is grave factual mistake, I regret. Nothing is perfect in this world. Also, my seniors or other batchmates may have Kohinoor or Cullinan diamonds of the experiences in their grey cells, but I could not keep my cards close to my chest and just shared my cultured pearls of wisdom.

Mumbai Customs function from New Customs House (NCH), Ballard Estate, Mumbai. This humongous and magnificent building was designed by an architect named George Wittett in Indo-Islamic Indian architecture, combined with the Gothic revival and Neo-Classical styles, favoured in Victorian

Britain. After the completion of the construction, it was opened for the transaction of the Custom business in 1924. Since then, the provisions of The Sea Customs Act-1978, The Land Customs Act 1924, The Inland Bonded Warehouses Act, 1896, and The Indian Tariff Act 1934, were being enforced from this very building and till the introduction of Customs Act in 1962. After enactment of The Customs Act 1962, this building continued to be the workplace of the people who came from every part India, including the staff at all levels of hierarchy, giving it the colour of mini-India. The work of Customs gradually increased manifold after the inception of Customs Act-62 and a need of bigger space was felt to handle the work load to run Mumbai Customs. So, in 1978-79, within the boundary of NCH, a 12 storied Annex Building was constructed connecting it to the main Building of New Customs House by two skywalk- pedways. It was inaugurated by a very efficient then Collector of Customs Shri J. P. Datta, who later became Chairman of CBEC in 1985. Now many sections, offices operate from the Annex building.

In this very New Customs House, I joined Mumbai Customs in 1986. Today when I look behind, I feel as if 28 years of my affiliation with this building and Mumbai Customs had passed in the blinks of eyes. So, I can recite the lines which I wrote at the start of this Book, meaning:

The pages of the book of my life turned over quickly like impulsive and rapid blinking of the eyes..

Thus, I accomplished my career in the Magnificent Mumbai Customs, encountering representative India ....

किताब -ए-जिंदगी के वरक पलटे ऐसे,
जैसे पलकें मेरी बेसाख्ता आमादगी से झपके....

बे-बहा मुम्बई कस्टम्स की मुलाजमत जैसे,
मुक्कमल की मैंने, नुमाइंदा भारत से रुबरु होके...